Merry Christmas
2001

from
Steve & Bobbie

AMERICA
Out of the Ashes

Honor Books
Tulsa, Oklahoma

2nd Printing

America Out of the Ashes
ISBN 1-56292-530-X
45-253-00250
Copyright © 2001 by Honor Books
P.O. Box 55388
Tulsa, Oklahoma 74155

Dedication

This book is dedicated to the victims, their families,
the survivors, and the American spirit of freedom.

*We in this country, in this generation,
are—by destiny rather than choice—
the watchmen on the walls of world
freedom. We ask, therefore, that we
may be worthy of our power and
responsibility, that we may exercise
our strength with wisdom and
restraint, and that we may achieve in
our time and for all time the ancient
vision of "peace on earth, good will
toward men." That must always be
our goal, and the righteousness of our
cause must always underlie our
strength. For as was written long ago:
"Except the Lord keep the city, the
watchman waketh but in vain."*

John F. Kennedy

Foreword

"Where was God?" Does that sound like a tough question to answer? It's one I've been asked a few times since the acts of terrorism on September 11. As a military officer, I might seem like a strange person to answer such a question. But God sometimes uses ordinary people to do extraordinary things, as you will soon see in this book, *America—Out of the Ashes*. But before we can do the extraordinary we must overcome the fear that stands before us. It is a giant, this "Formidable Fear", and we must slay him if we are to move forward in the weeks and months ahead.

On a recent flight following the terrorist attacks, I spoke to the passenger next to me who said, "I flew from DC to White Plains, New York, yesterday—I was the only person onboard." Fear is running in the streets, or more accurately, hiding in the houses.

All of us in the Pentagon greatly grieve the loss of those who died on that day, some who were colleagues of mine. Their loss is keenly felt, and they will be deeply missed. Additionally, I grieve the loss of the more than five thousand in New York. You may not have thought about it, but there are a lot more victims in New York than five thousand. There are the families, friends, and coworkers and, since 30 percent of American families are single-parent households, about 1800 children lost their primary parent and caregiver in New York. Some of them became orphans that day. "Where was God in all of this?" In answering that question, why don't we look at what *didn't* happen that *might* have happened that day.

The twin towers of the World Trade Center employed some 50,000 people, and though both buildings collapsed quickly after being struck, 90% survived. In the Pentagon, some 23,000 people were the target of the third plane. The latest count is about 189 lost their lives. More than 99% survived. The Pentagon section hit was the first of five sections to undergo renovations to strengthen and blast proof it from terrorist attacks and, as a result, saved untold lives.

The airplanes involved are another amazing story. We must begin by admitting our grief over the loss of the innocent lives that were taken by these terrorists. My neighbor came to my house, shaking, two days after the attacks. He was scheduled to be on the flight to Los Angeles along with five of his colleagues. At the last minute his boss called and told him he needed to go to Dallas instead. He got off the plane and is alive today. Sadly, his colleagues perished.

But where was God in this tragedy? Let's look at the flight manifests:

On American Airlines Flight 77, 289 seats were available, only 64 people were onboard. On American Airlines Flight 11, 251 seats were available, only 92 were onboard. On United Airlines Flight 175, 351 seats were available, only 65 were onboard.

Foreword

On United Airlines Flight 93, 289 seats were available, only 45 were onboard.

On Flight 93, the passengers of this fatally doomed plane stood up to their hijackers, resulting in crashing the plane into a deserted area in Pennsylvania. Their courage and willingness to stand up to "Formidable Fear" saved untold numbers of people and another Capitol area building. Their courage and success inspired the entire nation.

Out of a minimum of 75,000 potential "victims" that day, more than 93% survived or avoided these despicable acts. The buildings in New York probably should have collapsed immediately. Who held them up until tens of thousands could make it out? The Pentagon was hit at its strongest point, but it was nearly empty in those sections due to the renovations. Why did the plane hit those two sections?

Where was God? He was right where He was supposed to be—on the throne, and nothing was out of His sight. What was He doing? His work is clear in Jesus, who said, "I have come that they may have life, and that they may have it more abundantly." (John 10:10 NKJV).

So *there* was God, bringing life where the enemy had chosen massive destruction and death. Where was man? Some on September 11 had chosen to commit their lives to fulfilling their hatred in the cause of evil. God gave each of us the free will to choose our own path. God delivered some that day from death, and some were delivered into the presence of God himself. Are you ready for that moment?

During the Gulf War, I served as a Peacekeeper in Northern Israel. In my first week in Jerusalem, I was walking through Ben Yehuda Square. A terrorist bomb blew out a café into the middle of the mall, and the debris flew down both sides, knocking people, including me, to the ground. I tried to stand up and get out of the area, but the crowds had panicked and it was very difficult to get through. I wiped the dust off my clothes and was moving in the direction of King Herod's gate when two cars were set on fire with Molotov cocktails. The crowds continued to grow larger. In the middle of all of this chaos, an IDF (Israeli Defense Force) jeep, responding to the bomb, hit an 80-year-old Arab woman and killed her. By now the gathering crowds were so immense I could move only with the greatest of effort. They began to shake the jeep from side to side while shouting angrily at the Israeli soldiers inside. At that moment someone threw an explosive device at the jeep. I think it was a grenade of some kind, but I don't know for sure. The explosion injured many in the crowd as people with blood on their clothes pushed past me. I kept praying, and suddenly there was an opening in the crowd and I was able to escape. I walked up the hill and stumbled back to my hotel.

Where was God? He was on the throne, right where he was supposed to be. His Spirit was living in my heart, right where He was supposed to be. He heard my cry and opened a way. God didn't explode the bomb or set the cars on fire or kill the Arab woman or throw the grenade. That was man's doing. The more important question is, not where is God, but where are you? Where am I?

Some would say, "Six thousand perished in one hour; where was God?" God was working through the brave firefighters and policeman who rushed in to save the lives of others while losing their own. In doing so, they fulfilled the words of Christ, who said, "Greater love has no one than this, than to lay down one's life for his friends" (John 15:13 NKJV). We know where God was.

We also know where God was not. God was not in the hearts of those who chose murder over life and killed themselves along with thousands of innocent others. They chose hatred, and, sadly, it consumed many. Hatred is almost always fatal when it gets into the blood. It really doesn't matter what country you were born in or what language you speak—even what faith you claim to hold. When you let hatred take root and grow, there is no way to know how much destruction you will reap.

No, the question isn't so much where God is, but where you are. Have you taken the time, the way so many Americans did, to reassess your priorities in the wake of seeing the murder of innocents on September 11? God is speaking to you—each one of you. Yes, God is right where He is supposed to be. Are you?

Go home. If you have a spouse and children, hold them close. Call your family and tell them how much you love them. Begin to set your priorities right again if they've been off-center.

Will that extra hour at work really matter when you're seventy years of age looking back and assessing your life? Have you considered that the Lord may have an incredibly better plan for your life than any plan that you could design for yourself?

There are two paths before America. One is fear; and when fear is fully grown, it becomes "hatred". And hatred, given free reign, has the power to consume the entire world and all that live here. The other path is where you find God and the sacrificial love that He demonstrated for us in the person of Jesus Christ.

May we, as a nation, reflect; and in reflecting, choose; and in choosing, choose wisely: to humble ourselves, pray, seek God's face, and turn from the paths of death. Then we will see the light break out in our land again. Then we will see God heal our land, and, most importantly, forgive our sin.

May we, as a nation, choose *life*. God bless you all, and may the Lord cover and protect America.

"Colonel Jeff" O'Leary
United States Air Force
Author "Taking the High Ground:
Military Moments with God"
Founder and Director of Mission of Joy.

Introduction

Our world was shaken on Tuesday, September 11, 2001. Americans responded to this horrible tragedy as they have throughout history, with an outstretched hand. The unity of people across this land and the world has reached levels unknown to our generation.

Above all, this tragedy has reminded us of how fragile life is and how much we need God. The United States of America was founded on Godly principles by men and women who feared God and called upon Him for wisdom, direction, and freedom. Many laid down their lives in order to worship freely, and our forefathers even inscripted on our money "IN GOD WE TRUST".

We published *America Out of the Ashes* in order to help you, our readers, find comfort in the midst of the storm. We hope the stories we gathered touch your heart as they did ours. Stories of heroic acts, self-sacrifice, and courageous survival only confirm the indomitable spirit of the American people.

Our prayer is that God would encourage your heart as you read this book and that He would fulfill in you the hope of these words: ". . . to comfort all who mourn and provide for those who grieve . . . to bestow on them a crown of beauty instead of ashes, the oil of gladness instead of mourning, and a garment of praise instead of a spirit of despair." Isaiah 61:2,3 NIV

May God Bless America,

David V. Bordon
Executive Vice President / Publisher
Honor Books

Table of Contents

Table of Contents

Table of Contents

A Time for Prayer

A Timeline of Events

9-11-01

7:59 A.M.: American Flight 11 with ninety-two people leaves Boston's Logan Airport for Los Angeles.

8:01 A.M.: United Flight 93 with forty-five people leaves Newark Airport for San Francisco.

8:10 A.M.: American Flight 77 with sixty-four people leaves Washington's Dulles Airport for Los Angeles.

8:14 A.M.: United Flight 175 with sixty-five people leaves Boston for Los Angeles.

8:48 A.M.: Hijacked American Airlines Flight 11 crashes into the north tower of the World Trade Center.

9:06 A.M.: Hijacked United Airlines Flight 175 crashes into the south tower of the World Trade Center.

9:17 A.M.: The Federal Aviation Administration shuts down all New York City-area airports.

9:21 A.M.: The Port Authority of New York and New Jersey orders all bridges and tunnels into Manhattan closed.

9:31 A.M.:   President Bush, speaking in Sarasota, Florida, says the country has suffered an "apparent terrorist attack."

9:43 A.M.:   Hijacked American Airlines Flight 77 crashes into the Pentagon.

9:48 A.M.:   U.S. Capitol and White House's West Wing evacuated.

9:49 A.M.:   The FAA halts all flight operations at U.S. airports, the first time in U.S. history that national air traffic has been halted.

9:55 A.M.:   The south tower of the World Trade Center collapses.

9:57 A.M.:   President Bush departs from Florida.

10:08 A.M.:   Secret Service agents armed with automatic rifles are deployed into Lafayette Park across from the White House.

10:10 A.M.:   A portion of the Pentagon collapses.

10:10 A.M.:   Hijacked United Airlines Flight 93 crashes in a field in Somerset County, Pennsylvania.

10:13 A.M.:   The United Nations building in Manhattan evacuates, including 4,700 people from the headquarters building and 7,000 total from UNICEF and U.N. development programs.

10:22 A.M.:   The State and Justice departments and the World Bank in Washington, D.C. are evacuated.

10:24 A.M.:   The FAA reports that all inbound transatlantic aircraft flying into the United States are being diverted to Canada.

10:29 A.M.:   The north tower of the World Trade Center collapses.

10:45 A.M.:   All federal office buildings in Washington, D.C. are evacuated.

10.46 A.M.:   U.S. Secretary of State, Colin Powell, cuts short his trip to Latin America to return to the United States.

10.48 A.M.:   Police confirm the plane crash in Pennsylvania.

10:53 A.M.:   New York's primary elections, scheduled for Tuesday, are postponed.

10:54 A.M.:   Israel evacuates all diplomatic missions.

10:57 A.M.:   New York governor, George Pataki, announces that all state government offices are closed.

11:02 A.M.:   New York City mayor, Rudolph Giuliani, urges New Yorkers to stay at home and orders an evacuation of the area south of Canal Street.

11:18 A.M.:   American Airlines reports it has lost two aircraft: American Flight 11, a Boeing 767 flying from Boston to Los Angeles with eighty-one passengers and eleven crew aboard, and Flight 77, a Boeing 757 en route from Washington's Dulles International Airport to Los Angeles with fifty-eight passengers and six crew members aboard. Flight 11 slammed into the north tower of the World Trade Center. Flight 77 hit the Pentagon.

11:26 A.M.:   United Airlines reports that United Flight 93, en route from Newark, New Jersey, to San Francisco, California, has crashed in Pennsylvania. The airline also says that it is "deeply concerned" about United Flight 175.

11:59 A.M.:   United Airlines confirms that Flight 175, from Boston to Los Angeles, has crashed into the World

Trade Center's south tower with fifty-six passengers and nine crew members aboard.

12:04 P.M.: Los Angeles International Airport, the destination of three of the crashed airplanes, is evacuated.

12:15 P.M.: San Francisco International Airport is evacuated and shut down. The airport was the destination of United Airlines Flight 93, which crashed in Pennsylvania.

12:15 P.M.: The Immigration and Naturalization Service says U.S. borders with Canada and Mexico are on the highest state of alert, but no decision has been made about closing borders.

12:30 P.M.: The FAA says fifty flights are in U.S. airspace, but none are reporting any problems.

1:04 P.M.: From Barksdale Air Force Base in Louisiana, President Bush announces U.S. military on high alert worldwide, saying that all appropriate security measures are being taken. He asks for prayers for those killed or wounded in the attacks and says, "Make no mistake, the United States will hunt down and punish those responsible for these cowardly acts."

1:27 P.M.: A state of emergency is declared by the city of Washington.

1:44 P.M.: The Pentagon says five warships and two aircraft carriers will leave the U.S. Naval Station in Norfolk, Virginia, to protect the East Coast from further attack and to reduce the number of ships in port. The two carriers, the *USS George Washington* and the *USS John F. Kennedy,* are headed for the New York coast. The other ships headed to sea are frigates and guided missile destroyers capable of shooting down aircraft.

1:48 P.M.: President Bush leaves Barksdale Air Force Base aboard *Air Force One* and flies to an Air Force base in Nebraska.

2:30 P.M.: The FAA announces there will be no U.S. commercial air traffic until noon EST Wednesday at the earliest.

2:49 P.M.: At a news conference, Mayor Giuliani says that subway and bus service are partially restored in New York City. Asked about the number of people killed, Giuliani says, "I don't think we want to speculate about that—more than any of us can bear."

2:51 P.M.: Navy dispatches missile destroyers to New York and Washington, D.C.

3:07 P.M.: President Bush arrives at U.S. Strategic Command at Offutt Air Force Base in Nebraska.

3:55 P.M.: Karen Hughes, a White House counselor, says the president is at an undisclosed location, later revealed to be Offutt Air Force Base in Nebraska, and is conducting a National Security Council meeting by phone. Vice President Dick Cheney and National Security Adviser Condoleezza Rice are in a secure facility at the White House. Defense Secretary Donald Rumsfeld is at the Pentagon.

3:55 P.M.: Giuliani now says the number of critically injured in New York City is up to 200 with 2,100 total injuries reported.

4:06 P.M.: California governor, Gray Davis, dispatches urban search-and-rescue teams to New York City.

4:10 P.M.:   Building 7 of the World Trade Center complex is reported on fire.

4:25 P.M.:   The American Stock Exchange, the Nasdaq, and the New York Stock Exchange say they will remain closed Wednesday.

4:30 P.M.:   The president leaves Offutt Air Force Base in Nebraska aboard *Air Force One* to return to Washington.

5:25 P.M.:   The forty-seven-story Building 7 of the World Trade Center complex collapses. The evacuated building was damaged when the twin towers across the street collapsed earlier in the day. Other nearby buildings in the area remain ablaze.

5:30 P.M.:   U.S. officials say the plane that crashed in Pennsylvania could have been headed for one of three possible targets: Camp David, the White House, or the U.S. Capitol building.

6:00 P.M.:   Explosions are heard in Kabul, Afghanistan, hours after terrorist attacks targeted financial and military centers in the United States. The attacks occurred at 2:30 A.M. local time. Afghanistan is believed to be where Osama bin Laden, who U.S. officials say is possibly behind Tuesday's deadly attacks, is located. U.S. officials say later that the United States had no involvement in the incident whatsoever. The attack is credited to the Northern Alliance, a group fighting the Taliban in the country's ongoing civil war.

6:10 P.M.:   Giuliani urges New Yorkers to stay home Wednesday if they can.

6:40 P.M.:   U.S. Defense Secretary Rumsfeld holds a news conference in the Pentagon, noting the building is operational. "It will be in business tomorrow," he says.

A Timeline of Events

6:54 P.M.: President Bush arrives back at the White House aboard *Marine One* and is scheduled to address the nation at 8:30 P.M. The president landed earlier at Andrews Air Force Base in Maryland with a three-fighter jet escort.

7:17 P.M.: U.S. Attorney General, John Ashcroft, says the FBI is setting up a Web site for tips on the attacks: www.ifccfbi.gov. He also says family and friends of possible victims can leave contact information at 800-331-0075.

7:45 P.M.: The New York Police Department says that at least seventy-eight officers are missing. The city also says that as many as half of the first 400 firefighters on the scene were killed.

8:30 P.M.: President Bush addresses the nation, saying "thousands of lives were suddenly ended by evil" and asks for prayers for the families and friends of Tuesday's victims. "These acts shattered steel, but they cannot dent the steel of American resolve," he says. The president says the U.S. government will make no distinction between the terrorists who committed the acts and those who harbor them. He adds that government offices in Washington are reopening for essential personnel Tuesday night and for all workers Wednesday.

9:57 P.M.: Giuliani says New York City schools will be closed Wednesday and no more volunteers are needed for Tuesday evening's rescue efforts. He says there is hope that there are still people alive in the rubble. He also says that power is out on the westside of Manhattan and that health department tests show there are no airborne chemical agents about which to worry.

9-12-01

Nine survivors (three policeman and six firefighters) are found amidst the rubble of the World Trade Center.

New York Mayor Rudolph Giuliani warns death toll will be in the thousands.

President Bush labels attacks "acts of war" and asks Congress to find $20 billion to help rebuild and recover.

Officials confirm that a car believed to belong to hijackers has been confiscated in Boston, where two of the hijacked planes took off, and that it contained an Arabic language flight manual.

Investigators raid two Boston-area hotels believed to have been used by hijackers. Three suspects are detained but later released.

The United States deploys an air defense along the east and west coasts.

The FAA allows flights diverted by Tuesday's terrorist attacks to continue to their final destination.

Attorney General Ashcroft says the four planes "were hijacked by between three and six individuals per plane, using knives and box cutters, and in some cases making bomb threats." He also says a number of suspected hijackers were trained as pilots in the United States.

The North Atlantic Treaty Organization decides that Tuesday's terror strikes in the United States constitute an attack against all nineteen members, which commits them to respond militarily if they deem force is necessary to protect security.

The United Nations pulls staff out of Afghanistan.

9-13-01

Military recruiting skyrockets as patriotic Americans prepare for battle.

The Pentagon plans to call several thousand reservists to active duty.

A "national day of unity and mourning," is approved 100 to 0 by the Senate. The House later approves the resolution 408 to 0.

Secretary of Transportation, Norman Y. Mineta, announces new security precautions which airports and airlines will be required to implement. Security is increased to its highest level since the 1991 Gulf War.

Bond trading and futures activity resume. Stock markets remain closed for the longest stretch since World War II.

Defense Departments says about 190 people died in the attack at the Pentagon, including 64 aboard the hijacked plane.

The New York mayor announces that 4,763 people are missing.

Investigators find data recorder for United Flight 93 in Pennsylvania.

Secretary of State, Colin Powell, says Osama bin Laden is the prime suspect.

White House Press Secretary, Ari Fleischer, cites "real and credible information" that the plane which slammed into the Pentagon was originally intended to hit the White House.

9-14-01

President Bush declares a National Day of Prayer and Remembrance.

U.S. airlines resume operations and face difficulty with strict security rules, frightened passengers, and rapidly mounting financial problems.

NFL, Collegiate, and high school football games, as well as other major sports events, are canceled in the U.S.

Congress and White House officials give consent to military action in response to Tuesday's terrorist attacks and provide $40 billion package to aid retaliation and rebuilding, twice the amount President Bush had requested.

Americans of many faiths hold services and vigils to honor the victims. Bush and other dignitaries gather for service at National Cathedral in Washington.

Searchers find flight data and voice recorders of hijacked plane that crashed into the Pentagon.

Authorities make their first arrest in the investigation: one of the men detained at New York's Kennedy Airport is arrested as a material witness.

President Bush arrives in New York City to see the site of the former World Trade Center.

9-15-01

President Bush meets with his national security advisers at the presidential retreat Camp David and afterward, for the first time, singles out suspected terrorist Osama bin Laden as a "prime suspect" in Tuesday's attacks.

Coast Guard cutters patrol ports and waterways at unprecedented levels from New York harbor to San Diego.

F-15 Eagles and *F-16 Fighting Falcons* fly combat patrols over Washington, New York, and other major cities.

President Bush signs an order authorizing Pentagon officials to call up 35,000 Reserves.

9-16-01

Funeral and memorial services begin for firefighters and individuals who died in Tuesday's attack.

9-17-01

Wall Street reopens for the first time since the previous week's terrorist attacks.

The Federal Reserve cuts interest rates by half a percentage point.

9-18-01

One week after the attack, the nation pauses at 8:45 A.M. EST for a moment of silence in honor of the victims.

Media reports that over fifty countries lost citizens in the World Trade Center attack.

9-19-01

The media informs the country that American warplanes began flying overseas from U.S. bases yesterday as the Pentagon ordered dozens of fighters, bombers, and other aircraft to the Persian Gulf, Indian Ocean, and—in an unprecedented move—the two former Soviet republics of Uzbekistan and Tajikistan.

The *USS Theodore Roosevelt* aircraft carrier leaves from the pier at Naval Station Norfolk headed to the Mediterranean, then to the Persian Gulf.

A Time for Heroes

*Heroism is endurance for one moment
more.*

George Kennan

Meant for a Higher Purpose

He wasn't supposed to be on Flight 93, but his flight the day before had been cancelled. Jeremy Glick hadn't even wanted to go, but his wife, Lyzbeth, had told him that going was his duty to his company. As he boarded the plane, he called to say goodbye, but Lyz was asleep, having been up with the baby. His father-in-law took the call.

An hour later, Jeremy called again to talk to Lyz. He needed to tell her that his plane had been hijacked by three men in red headbands with ceramic knives. The men, who seemed Arabic, had taken over the cockpit and had moved part of the passengers to the back of the plane. Jeremy had heard from another passenger who had spoken to his wife that the World Trade Center had been hit. But he wanted to hear it from Lyz's mouth. As Lyz told Jeremy the news, her mother, Joanne, called 911 on her cell phone. The New York Trooper's Barracks patched in and relayed questions through Joanne's connection.

The phone call lasted twenty minutes as Jeremy collected information and answered questions relayed through Lyz.

"The hijackers say they have a bomb," Jeremy quietly informed her. Upon hearing the gasp of fear over the line, he told his wife, "Be brave, Lyz. Be brave." He told her many times that he loved her and that she was to take care of Emmy, their daughter. He gave Lyz instructions to make the decisions in her own life that would make her happy. "I need you to be happy," he said, indicating with these words that he knew there was a strong probability that he would not survive.[1]

As Jeremy Glick and the other passengers realized how the other planes had been used, they began to formulate a plan. Jeremy, a 6'4", well-built Judo champion, kept his wife informed of the deliberations between him and a few other men who were also tall and willing to fight.

Then the time came for the hijacked men to make what would be the most important decision in their lives: to attack or not. "But what about their guns?" Lyz asked. Jeremy assured her that the three red-headbanded men only had knives. "You do what you feel you need to do," Lyz replied, in an unprecedented resolute voice.

As his fellow passengers voted, he announced to Lyz and the New York Troopers on the line that they had decided to attack. Time and time again in those drawn out moments, he had realized that his hijackers might use the plane as more than a hostage for negotiations: more people might be killed than just those on board. He didn't want that to happen and told Lyz so.

Then he told her to hold the phone because he would be right back. But Lyz could listen no longer. She handed the phone to her father, who heard screams, then more screams that were muffled and far away. Then nothing.

Meant for a Higher Purpose

His father-in-law, Richard Makely, called Jeremy Glick a hero. Yes, he was. He was the kind of hero who made a choice that preserved the lives of others even when he knew he might not live through it. He and the other men prevented the hijackers from using the airplane to attack another site in Washington D.C., possibly the White House or the Capitol. Instead, the plane crashed in a remote area of Pennsylvania.

Later in an interview, Jeremy's wife, Lyz, stated, "I think just with, you know, all the badness that's been going on, that . . . God or some higher power knew that Jeremy had the strength to somehow stop some of the bad that was going on. I believe that. I believe that Jeremy was meant for a higher purpose."[2]

We must be willing, individually and as a nation, to accept whatever sacrifices may be required of us. A people that values its privileges above its principles soon loses both.

Dwight D. Eisenhower

[1] © National Broadcasting Company, Inc. 2001. All Rights Reserved.
[2] Ibid.

Let's Roll

"Todd was an ordinary guy," says Lisa Beamer. "He was extraordinary to me and to his family, but to the world he was ordinary. And like any ordinary guy getting on a plane that day in a business suit, he was able to do extraordinary things."

Lisa Beamer's husband, Todd, left Newark airport last Tuesday morning on United Flight 93, bound for San Francisco. He was supposed to have left the day before for his business meeting, but decided to spend an extra night at home with his wife and two young sons.

Shortly after 10 A.M., while Lisa was watching television with a friend at her home in New Jersey, the jet crashed in a Pennsylvania field, killing all forty-four on board.

"I was standing behind my couch, I'll always remember, when I heard them say that was the United flight from Newark to San Francisco that just went down," says Lisa. "And I said, that's his flight. And my friend said, 'No, he might be on a different one, he might not have made it on the plane.' And I just said 'No, I know that's his flight,' and I just said no.'"

Authorities now believe 32-year-old Todd Beamer and other passengers died trying to overpower the hijackers. In doing so, they may have prevented a much greater catastrophe—the terrorists had turned the plane toward Washington, D.C.

Three days later, Lisa found out how the authorities knew that her husband had gone down fighting.

"My contact at United whom I'd been speaking with multiple times a day all week called Friday night and said, 'I'd like you to go somewhere quiet,'" says Lisa. "And I said, 'What could be worse? What news could be worse than what you've already given me?' And I went with my brother up in my bedroom and we got on the phone and [the contact] said, 'I received a correspondence from GTE Airfone that one of their operators spoke to Todd during the hijacking.' And then he gave me her phone number, which she included. And on Saturday morning I called her at her home."

Lisa Beamer called another Lisa — an Airfone operator for GTE named Lisa Jefferson who had already told investigators about her conversation with Todd in the last harrowing moments aboard the hijacked plane.

But when the operator picked up the phone and asked if she were Lisa Beamer, "I could barely get those words out and it seemed like she was just waiting to talk to me," says Lisa. "Obviously, I didn't have to describe who I was. She knew right away."

The conversation began. "She told me that when Todd initially called, he called at 9:45 in the morning," says Lisa. "He gave her his flight information and said, 'We're being hijacked.' He described the hijackers. He said that there were three. He didn't know their nationality. He knew that two had knives and one had some sort of an apparatus strapped around his waist with a red belt so that, that appeared to be a bomb."

Then he told the operator where he was on the plane. "What he said happened is that they had left the first class cabin, ten people up there. And then they moved twenty-seven people who were in the rear of the plane to be seated all the way at the back. The hijackers had removed the pilots from the cabin and had entered the cabin and closed the door. I think two of them had gone into the cabin and closed the door, and he knew that the pilot and co-pilot were injured. He did not know if they were dead or alive."

But it quickly became clear to Todd that soon they would all be dead.

"It seemed like after a while he realized either from information from other passengers or because the plane started flying more erratically, that this was not going to end well," says Lisa.

She wasn't sure at that point if a plan was being formulated. "Initially, when he said that he knew he wasn't going to make it, what he did was he told her about our family, and he told her about me," says Lisa. "And she knew the boys' names. And she knew we were expecting a baby in January. And he gave her our phone number and said, 'I need you to call Lisa. Please promise that you'll do that for me and let her know how much I love her and the boys.' And I didn't need to hear that, but I knew in my heart that would be the sentiment. But it was great to get that message from him three days later."

A fter he covered his family, he asked her to pray the Lord's Prayer with him.

Operator Lisa Jefferson promised to relay his words. "She followed through. And then after he covered his family, he asked her to pray the Lord's Prayer with him. And she did that. And then he asked Jesus to help him. You know, in the Lord's Prayer, it asks us to forgive our trespasses as we forgive those who trespass against us. And in some way, he was forgiving those people for what they were doing, the most horrible thing you could ever do to someone. But after he had gone through that process and made sure that we were going to be taken care of as best he could, he told her that he and some of the other passengers—he specifically mentioned Jeremy Glick—were going to jump on the hijacker with the bomb. And the next thing she heard Todd say was, 'Are you ready? Let's roll.' And as soon as I heard her say, 'Let's roll,' I got a smile on my face because I knew that was Todd's voice. We use that phrase all the time with our boys. It's kind of hard to corral little boys sometimes. But when we say, 'Let's roll, boys,' they head to the door and they start to get ready and, you know, get ready for the next thing we're going to do. And he said—'Let's roll'—just like he did so many times at our home. And [the operator] said after that, she didn't hear anything more from Todd. That was 10 A.M. So he was on the phone for fifteen minutes."

Lisa knows there were sounds of struggle, according to the operator. "Yes, she said there were screams. She said there was a lot of commotion and there were screams. And she said she stayed on the line, and it became silent then. But she stayed on until she heard that the plane had crashed about 10 minutes later."

After hearing about the phone call, Lisa felt relief. "You know, it was just a blessing because people had asked me, you know, do you think Todd was involved?" says Lisa. "What do you think Todd did? And everybody who knows Todd said, 'Oh Todd was there.' Todd was, you know, he was at the forefront. He was on this team that was going to take down these hijackers. Because Todd was a competitor. He wasn't an aggressive person, but he certainly was a person who would stand up for himself and stand up for other people. And he would not go down without a fight."

Two Lisas, not one, have been forever changed within those long minutes.

"[Lisa Jefferson] said that she held it together during the phone call for him, and she said she lost it when she got off," says Lisa. "And I told her what a rock she must have been for Todd and what a comfort she must have been for Todd in those last minutes. And she said in those minutes she talked to Todd, she felt like she made a friend for life. And I said, you know, I'm sure that he felt the same way."

David Beamer, Todd's father, was on business in California when he got the news about his son. He drove across the country to be with his family.

"I think our son handled the situation admirably. I knew in my heart of hearts that Todd would have acted the way that he did," says David. "And [his act confirmed it] for the rest of the world, to understand what these men, the many heroes on this flight did give us— . . . a piece of comfort. And I think it sets an example for what I fear many other Americans are going to be called upon to do."

At a memorial service for Todd Beamer on Sunday, healing words and fond memories were shared for the man who loved to say, "Let's roll!"

"But we know he loves us, and he still loves us," says Lisa. "And I just have so many people who are going to be able to share their memories of Todd with them through the years. So I think [his children] are going to get to know their dad. And they're going to want to be like him one day. And I'm going to make sure of that. Todd made us proud of him, and we're going to make him proud, too."

> *"A tragedy like this could have torn our country apart. But instead it has united us, and we have become a family."*
>
> Rev. Billy Graham

'He's Given Me the Rest of My Life!'

Retired Navy officer Jerry Henson never expected sitting at a desk managing counter-drug operations to be a dangerous activity, after having flown seventy-two combat reconnaissance missions over Vietnam, dodging enemy fire, and manuevering short aircraft carrier runways. He had always come home safely without injuries. But when American Airlines Flight 77 crashed into the Pentagon where he sat, Henson once again sensed danger.

First, there was the impact. Then, the lights went out. Finally, everything around him began to fall. Henson, sideways behind his desk, was trapped at the waist under some immovable weight. As he and his trapped coworkers called for help, the flames crept closer and closer. Yet no one responded to their calls.

Then Henson saw the soot-covered boots nearing his broken body. A rescuer had found him and was able to carry him to safety and medical assistance. But the rescuer had doubts that he would ever see Jerry Henson alive again.

Four days later, Henson was miraculously discharged from the hospital to continue healing at home. His one goal: to find the unknown rescuer who had saved his life. "I just want to thank him profoundly because he's the reason I'm here . . . he's given me the rest of my life," Henson told reporters.

A few days later, *Dateline NBC* reporters successfully located Henson's rescuer. His name, Lt. Commander David Tarantino. Jerry Henson's deepest wish had been answered. After thanking Tarantino for his help, Henson's wife hugged the hero who had brought her husband out of the ruins into her arms. "God love you!" she said, looking into his tired eyes.

Jerry Henson assured Tarantino one last time, "I had planned to spend whatever time it took the rest of my life to find you." Thank goodness, it wasn't necessary to spend an entire lifetime searching. Thank God, two more lifetimes will go on.

Heroism feels and never reasons and therefore is always right.

Anonymous

A Hero in Life

A hero is born in one glorious moment, but he or she trains for a lifetime.

Father Mychal Judge lived like a hero before his death revealed him as one to the rest of the world. A priest and a friar, Father Judge devoted himself to people. They knew him from the soup kitchen where he helped alongside his order, the Franciscans. To the firefighters of Ladder 24, he'd been a firehouse chaplain for ten years, eating meals with them, living across the street from the firehouse in the friary, throwing on his uniform and hat to race off to fires with them. He prayed with the fire victims as well as for the firefighters who helped them.

On the morning of September 11, 2001, when he heard of the plane crashing into the World Trade Center, Father Judge, even at sixty-eight years of age, never hesitated to perform his solemn duties as he threw on his fireproof uniform and raced to the site. Giving a blessing to a group of firefighters as they went into the building, he then proceeded to the street so he could administer last rites to a fireman who had been killed by the body of a falling woman. But he never got to speak a word. As he took off his hat to begin the rites he knew so well, he was killed by a piece of falling debris.

Though Father Judge was a patriotic American known for choosing "God Bless America" to close the services he presided over, the world, not Ladder 24, was his parish. In 1998, 1999, and 2000, he had traveled to Ireland to encourage reconciliation. Father Judge toiled beside the homeless, the drug addicts, the dying AIDS patients, and anyone who crossed his path. So it wasn't surprising to all who knew him that he was ministering at the time of his death. Father Mychal Judge became a hero in one tragic moment but had trained a hero's life for a lifetime. Neither death nor life could catch him being anything else.

I wish to make an earnest call to everyone, Christians and the followers of other religions, that we work together to build a world without violence, a world that loves life and grows in justice and solidarity; we must not let what has happened lead to a deepening of divisions. Religion must never be used as a reason for conflict.

Pope John Paul II

Saving a Life and a Bride

By Edie Magnus

A mid the avalanche of bleak news from ground zero at the World Trade Center, there are some scattered bright spots, moments of light punctuating the days of darkness.

It was an island of hope in a sea of chaos. NYU downtown medical center, the hospital closest to the World Trade Center, was keeping order amid the madness.

"This is in every way comparable to what you see in a war on a battlefield," says Dr. Howard Beaton, chief of surgery and emergency services.

That first night a *Dateline* producer followed Dr. Beaton as he went from bed to bed in the Intensive Care Unit. It is where life hangs in the balance.

"This is where we stabilize people," says Dr. Beaton.

One of the first victims brought in minutes after the attack was a young woman who appeared to be in her late 20s. "This woman was identified originally as Jane Doe #1—she was injured when the first plane struck," says Dr. Beaton.

In the emergency room, Dr. Jerry Ginsburg, a plastic surgeon, found Jane Doe #1 hanging to life by a thread.

> I said to myself "What is she going to do with these feet?"

"We put intravenous fluids into her, and essentially took this lady who was absolutely bleeding to death, stabilized her so that I could bring her to the OR [operating room]," says Dr. Ginsburg. "Her legs were almost cut off, almost completely cut off."

They were cut off apparently by debris falling to the street.

"We've been told that what hit her was the landing gear of the plane," says Dr. Beaton. "If it had been a few inches forward it would have hit her in the head and she would have never made it here."

The trauma team operating on Jane Doe had few options and even less time. Her legs, they concluded, should be amputated—and fast.

"One of our superb surgeons came in—well trained in trauma—and he looked at the four of us in the team and said, in his Australian accent, 'for God sakes, cut them off, we've got to get going,'" says Dr. Ginsburg. "And that was actually superb trauma training. You don't waste time on things that are non-reconstructable, you save the blood, you get the job done."

But one surgical team member, a foot specialist, begged for more time before going through with the amputation.

"And Dr. Botwinick said, 'I'm going to go a little bit slowly, I think I can save these feet,'" says Dr. Ginsburg.

Surgeons worked for hours, slowly and meticulously reconstructing her lower torso, her legs and feet.

"As I'm operating on her and I'm looking at her," says Dr. Ginsburg, "I said it's not Jane Doe #1, it's somebody with long, dark, gorgeous hair, probably late 20s or 30, and I said to myself 'What is she going to do with these feet?' Here I'm reconstructing this woman, and I'm dying to know who is Jane Doe #1?"

Remarkably they were able to save her feet and legs. But when she came out of surgery, the team still had no idea who this woman was.

About eight hours later, despite the tube down her throat, she whispered her name and phone number.

"When I got her name and phone number and I spoke to her fiancé who answered the phone," says Dr. Ginsburg, "I heard the word 'fiancé,' and I said to myself, she's going to dance at her wedding on her own feet, and not on prosthesis."

At home on New York's Upper West Side, Greg St. John had been frantic for hours, unable to find the woman he was to marry a year from this month. Then his phone rang.

"I waited about eight hours through the day until the surgeons called me and they asked if I would know a Jane Doe #1, they think it's a Debbie," says St. John.

He says it was the best phone call of his life.

It turns out, Jane Doe #1 is 30-year-old Debbie Manderfield from Manhattan. Four days after nearly losing her life. Debbie was finally able to breathe on her own, to talk— although her voice was just a whisper.

She said she was getting married next September. "I have an amazing fiancé. He is one of those few special people in life that I know I found a truly unique and vibrant person."

Debbie told *Dateline* that on Tuesday she had gone to work early at the American Express office in the World Trade Center.

"What I remember is walking out of the subway into the street and seeing the top of one of the buildings on fire, and I said that can't be true," says Manderfield. "And I then I saw the other tower explode, and I knew I had to run for my life, and that's all I remember."

Debbie's recovery will be long and slow, but she's off to a start that's nothing short of amazing, thanks to the helping hands of strangers who have now become lifelong friends.

"I can say I am so thrilled and so impressed with the people who have spent time with me," says Manderfield. "They have changed my life all for the better, and I love them. I don't want to lose touch with you, you didn't have to go to this extent."

"She's in ICU a day after this amazing trauma," says Dr. Ginsburg. "She's had 30 units of blood. She has a tube between her vocal chords and can't speak. [She'd had this] devastating injury and the fact that we've changed the shape of her backside and she was desperate to get a tablet and writes to me, 'So doc, my butt's smaller?' And I said, 'My kind of woman.'"

"It was unbelievable to have her open her eyes and smile at me," says a nurse who helped care for Manderfield. "As soon as she opened her eyes, she wouldn't let go of me, and we both started crying. She's going to live, and we're going to her wedding."

Everything can be taken from a man but one thing: The last of human freedoms—to choose one's attitude in any given set of circumstances—to choose one's own way.

Viktor Frankel

Fire Chief
Ray Downey

ravery is the first thing we think of in firefighters. But New York City's fire chief of special operations, Ray Downey, is hailed by his peers as the smartest firefighter on a force full of smart firefighters. Few men can enter a burning building and see order. Downey can. Few men can walk through the wake of chaos, be it a hurricane's wrath or a terrorist's bomb, and know how to organize and proceed. Downey can.

We use the present tense, not out of foolish optimism, but out of respect. Firefighters aren't dead until their bodies are found; for now, Downey is unaccounted for. On Tuesday, September 11, 2001, Downey, 63, a father of five, including two New York City firefighters, did what thirty-nine years of experience had taught him to do best. He arrived at an emergency and sprang into action. By several accounts, Downey moved toward the rubble of the first tower, hoping to save some of those trapped underneath. He had to have known the odds. A few months ago, he spoke about the funerals of three beloved firefighters. "You say to yourself, 'Not me.' But when the unexpected happens, there's nothing you can do about it." When the second tower collapsed, Downey disappeared.

Downey is the most decorated firefighter in the department, and that isn't even at the top of his résumé. He headed the search-and-rescue efforts at the World Trade Center bombing in 1993, the Oklahoma City bombing in 1995, and the TWA Flight 800 explosion in 1996. He volunteered to coordinate a rescue effort after a hurricane hit the Dominican Republic and served on the Gilmore Commission, a congressional advisory panel that last year issued a report entitled "Toward a National Strategy for Combating Terrorism." The man knows disaster.

He also knows what he signed up for. Speaking at another firefighter's funeral, this one less than two weeks ago, Downey said, "We have to accept this as part of the job. Sometimes in this job, good-bye really is good-bye."

Freedom is still expensive. It still costs money. It still costs blood. It still calls for courage and endurance, not only in soldiers, but in every man and woman who is free and who is determined to remain free.

Harry S Truman

Captain Pat Brown

C aptain Pat Brown, 48, always said the New York City fire department had saved his life. He came home to Queens from Vietnam in 1973 covered with medals but angry and choked up on adrenaline, daring anyone to knock the chip off his shoulder. Not good qualities for most jobs — unless you need to suit up every day against an adversary like fire. He made some spectacular rescues, including a courageous save as a lieutenant in 1991 on the roof of a midtown office building: Brown and two of his men held an inch-thick rope in their bare hands and, straining and skidding toward the parapet, lowered two firefighters, one at a time, down into black, billowing smoke; each man grabbed a panicky victim from a windowsill perch. The lunchtime crowd below went wild with relief.

Brown eventually became one of the most decorated members in the history of the department. Women were attracted by the face, the Cagney voice, and the "hero" who made the papers — including the time he chased down a mugger in Central Park during his workout. But he was restless. Brown, who never married, gave up drinking and late nights to read up on religion, get a black belt in karate, learn yoga. He volunteered as a self-defense teacher for the blind. The honors and citations didn't mean what they once did, as he watched mentors and protégés die in fires. Still, he loved fire fighting. Last Tuesday, his company got the call to go to the World Trade Center. Firefighter Brandon Gill says someone yelled, "Don't go in there, Paddy!" but Brown called back, "Are you nuts? We've got a job to do!" and rushed up the stairs of the north tower with his men, past the engine companies with their hoses, to look for trapped office workers. Said Gill: "One of the newspapers called him 'the gallant Captain Pat Brown.' That's exactly what he was."

I have been asked hundreds of times in my life why God allows tragedy and suffering. I have to confess that I really do not know the answer. I have to accept, by faith, that God is a God of love and mercy and compassion in the midst of suffering. The Bible says God is not the author of evil.

Billy Graham

She Saved My Life

F or a few brief moments on Tuesday morning, Irish architect Ronnie Clifford, 47, was twice blessed: as both hero and survivor of the terrorist attacks. Standing in the lobby of the Marriott Hotel after the first plane hit, Clifford saw a charred woman rise from the pyre, her fingernails melting off and her clothes burned onto her skin. He was shielding her with his coat when a second shudder sent them to the floor. To keep her from drifting off, they conversed and prayed. She told him her name, Jennieann Maffeo, and the name and number of her boss at Paine Webber; she also told him she was asthmatic and allergic to latex. Clifford took copious notes. With the help of a Marriott employee and oxygen from the hotel's medical kit, Clifford led her to the nearest ambulance. Maffeo's charred skin still clinging to his coat, Clifford ran west and hopped on a ferry back to his home in Glen Ridge, New Jersey, where he hugged his wife and daughter, who was celebrating her eleventh birthday on September 11.

Only then did he learn he was also thrice cursed. He had lost family members: Clifford's sister, Ruth McCourt, 45, and his niece Juliana, 4, had been aboard the United Airlines flight that plowed through 2 World Trade Center. He had also lost a family friend: Paige Farley Hackel, 46, who was meeting McCourt in Los Angeles but traveling separately on the American Airlines flight that crashed into the other tower. Hackel, a spiritual counselor, was heading to Los Angeles for a seminar with Deepak Chopra. McCourt was taking her daughter on a surprise trip to Disneyland.

In the midst of his own grief, Clifford found the number of Maffeo's boss and called to say she was alive but in very bad shape. Her boss then contacted the family, who eventually found her in critical condition at New York-Presbyterian Hospital, burned over so much of her body that the doctors required the family to put on scrubs before seeing her. When they were finally reunited, Maffeo insisted that they track down the man who saved her.

> **"The truth is, she saved my life; she gave me strength."**

Consoling his brother-in-law in Connecticut and his family back in Ireland, Clifford received a phone call from Maffeo's sister. Clifford told her about his own losses in the crash. The sister gave Clifford the family's thanks for putting himself at risk to be her sister's savior. Clifford replied that she had it wrong — he never would have made it out of the building before it collapsed if he had not picked up her sister. "The truth is, she saved my life; she gave me strength," says Clifford. He also believes his sister Ruth's hovering spirit pointed his way out of the carnage.

Even though I walk through the valley of the shadow of death, I will fear no evil, for you are with me; your rod and your staff, they comfort me.

Psalm 23:4

"You Have to Help"

One of the greatest frustrations for Americans watching the news and hearing about the tragedy at the World Trade Towers and at the Pentagon was the desire to do something to help. So many volunteers showed up in New York that many had to be turned away. In some cities, people overwhelmed the blood banks. They stood in long lines to give blood and to satisfy that longing to do something, anything to help. Many were asked to return later—there was enough blood for now.

By the middle of Tuesday, Washington Hospital Center announced a pressing need for human skin transplants for seven patients who had been burned in the Pentagon bombing. Texas was the location of the skin bank closest to the Washington hospital. The director of the Transplant Services Center at the University of Texas, Ellen Heck, was willing to help, but she faced several obstacles. First, the airports were shut down. Second, she couldn't arrange with the Air Force, the Federal Emergency Management Agency, and the Texas National Guard to get the perishable skin to the place it was needed.

After she made the decision to have it driven up to Washington by car, she was faced with the third difficulty—

keeping the frozen skin at the right temperature for a long drive north and east of Texas. She had the skin stored in pouches of liquid nitrogen laid on a bed of dry ice in three Styrofoam coolers and asked for volunteers. These two, Matthew Harris and Eddie Perryman, had been the first to raise their hands. Ellen supplied them with an extra pair of scrubs, a bag of mints, and Tootsie Rolls to snack on with credit cards and cash for gas and food.

Harris said later, "You have to do something. You have to help. I'm shocked, and I'm angry. But this is what I'm able to do—dropping everything and travelling 1,328 miles for something desperately needed."

His partner agreed, "I've always wanted a chance to help. Unfortunately, it came at a time like this."

While en route, Harris and Perryman had to stop at hospitals to resupply the necessary dry ice. This was the longest trip they had ever made to deliver skin or corneas. Though the urgency to speed presented a continuous temptation, they kept the speedometer under control. Matthew and Eddie rolled into the Washington Hospital grounds, 1,328 miles later, to deliver their cargo. Physically and emotionally exhausted, they rested in confidence. They had helped America, in some small way, survive her crisis.

> *They helped every one his neighbour; and* **every one** *said to his brother, Be of good courage.*
>
> Isaiah 41:6 KJV

Company of Heroes

By Sally Jenkins

F irefighters are easy to love. They don't give out tickets, or make arrests, or pump too many bullets into vestibules. They are dashing, in those sloped helmets and suspenders, and they are good-natured. In this town, anyway, they have now become the ultimate celebrities, the model of what makes a hero, and the measure of what's admirable and desirable.

Caps with the initials FDNY have started turning up in store windows. People flock to the firehouses and wait outside, like groupies, to see a firefighter. Crowds collect on West Street and spontaneously applaud as they come trudging up out of the wreckage site like spectral figures, covered in gray ash.

At the Engine 24, Ladder 5 firehouse on Sixth Avenue and Houston Street, a woman walked up to firefighter Carmine Evola and threw her arms around him and hugged him. All of his old girlfriends have started calling again.

"I'm going to have to start wearing this shirt when I'm off duty," he said.

Out: dot-com geeks. In: burly men with axes.

Out: dot-com geeks.
In: burly men with axes.

That "Gladiator" Australian actor—or any of the Hollywood types— is suddenly doughy and pallid compared to a New York firefighter. Because these firemen are "the real things."

Their ears bled. Their hats smoked. Their boots melted to their feet. A volunteer physician, Mark Cerezin, spent two days in triage caring for their roasted appendages. He describes cutting the heavy rubber away from their bare feet.

"Their boots were melted like marshmallows on a stick," he said.

After touring the attack site and talking with the firemen, President Bush said, as if it had just occurred to him, "These are the men who will fight our wars." That's true, as New Yorkers now know better than anybody—these are the kind of men who fight all our wars. Mayor Rudolph Giuliani said, "These men are fighting the first battle."

Last Saturday night four firefighters walked into the White Horse Tavern. The firefighters wore turnout coats smeared with grime, and swoop-brimmed helmets and ash-caked boots. As they moved past the button-down brokers and bearded intellectuals sitting at tables on the sidewalk, a wave of cheers began. By the time they reached their table, the crowd was screaming, pounding on the scarred wooden tables, chanting, "USA! USA!"

On a train into Manhattan from Connecticut, the commuters read their Wall Street Journals. As they pulled into the station, the conductor said, "Everyone have a safe and good day. We have a couple of firefighters on board today. Let's thank them." The train resounded with clapping.

Evola says, "You can't walk a block in uniform without people saying thank you."

They walked into buildings where they did not work, and restaurants where they could not afford to eat, to save people who might have looked down on them.

"This is a nice upper-middle-class neighborhood," Evola says. "Before, maybe their noses were a little up in the air. Now they're looking at us, waving, talking to us."

The firefighters who serve Manhattan can't afford to live in it. They live in Staten Island, or Queens, or the Bronx, or New Jersey. Evola has been a firefighter for nineteen years and his take-home pay, after taxes, is $760 every two weeks. Most firefighters moonlight as bartenders or security guards or construction workers.

A week after the disaster, the survivors from Engine 24 have finally started to wander back into Chumley's, a famed old speakeasy on Barrow Street once known for harboring authors and poets. It's particularly a favorite haunt of the men of Engine 24, Ladder 5. "They come in after a couple of days straight down there, and they're losing their minds," Schlopak says. The managers and customers don't applaud when they walk in. They note the glassy eyes and keep a respectful silence. "Thank God," someone murmurs.

"Everyone just hugs them, and shuts up," says Meredith Darcy, Chumley's manager.

One window of Chumley's is a piece of stained glass glazed with the emblem of the ladder company. An old red call box is bolted to the wall, as is other firehouse memorabilia.

The owner, Steve Schlopak, has hung a framed portrait of a famous department hero, Capt. John Drennan, who perished with two other men in 1994 when he was fighting a fire inside a building and a gas cloud exploded. Drennan was so tough that he lived for forty days with fourth-degree burns over most of his body.

It was he who best described a firefighter's duty: "Two hundred and twenty days of boredom, and twenty minutes a year of sheer terror." One of the men missing in the World Trade wreckage is Drennan's best friend, Capt. Pat Brown. "When they find Pat Brown, they'll find him in the densest place, in the highest part of the building, with the most firefighters around him," Schlopak predicted.

Here is a little of what they did to get all this attention.

When the first hijacked aircraft hit Tower 1 of the 110-story twin skyscrapers, Fire Chief Peter Ganci yelled down the hall to his commanders, "Look out your windows, the World Trade

Center's been hit by a plane!" The men rose, looked, and lunged for their gear.

Ganci, too, pulled on his turnout coat. He was no desk-bound bureaucrat. His dress uniform was covered with medals for pulling people out of burning buildings. He was also an old-school fireman who loved to sit in the firehouse kitchens, the social center of firefighter life where they cook extravagant meals for each other. He always gave new firefighters two pieces of advice:

"When you walk out the door in the morning, don't let your wife see how happy you are to go to work," and "Never tell your wife how good the station house food is. If she asks, tell her you had hot dogs."

Somebody said that when Ganci looked at a fire, he wore a look of defiance, a sneer, that said, "I've got you. You're not going to get me."

So Ganci, like every other firefighter in the city, raced toward the site. Coming on the 9 A.M. shift, getting off—they all jumped on the trucks together. So did the retirees, and the men on medical leave who happened to be hanging around the station houses. One group of firefighters commandeered a crowded 67th Street crosstown bus.

Ganci established a command center. Then he realized the towers weren't stable. "Everyone back!" he yelled. "We're moving north! Go now!"

But a lot of his men were still inside. They couldn't hear him. So he ran south. "He didn't have a reverse gear," said Paul Nigro, his deputy. No one saw him alive again. "Every firefighter at the scene, more than 500 people, went directly into the most dangerous conditions they had ever seen," said Nigro.

Thirty-four are confirmed to have been killed. More than 300 are still missing.

Firefighters arriving at the Trade Center after the towers' collapse looked through the ashen twilight and saw something they probably hadn't seen before: near the mountains of wreckage sat a half-dozen smashed and charred fire trucks. Their ladders were torn and twisted like cheap dinner forks.

More fires broke out as they worked. Everything around them seemed to burn, or move, or collapse. Their eyes began to swell shut from the smoke and debris. They tore and sprained their ankles or knees climbing through the burning heap. Medical personnel washed out their eyes and bandaged their arms and legs, and tried to make them come out, but none of them would. Dr. Edward Casey treated one firefighter who'd been thrown by a blast and badly sprained his ankle. Casey bandaged the injury and told him, "You're discharged, go *home.*" The firefighter said, "Give me my turnout coat. I'm not going home as long as my company's in there."

Three days later, at Ganci's funeral in St. Kilian Church in the suburb of Farmingdale, N.Y., one of Ganci's sons, Chris, rose and addressed the mourners. "His actions might have spared someone else's son from making this speech today," he said.

Compounding the grief was the fact that the term "brotherhood" in the fire department is not just a metaphor.

Some of the old Irishmen in the department call it "square rooting": everyone is someone's son or brother or cousin. Jimmy Boyle, the retired president of the firefighter's union, lost his son Michael, who was with Engine 33. Kevin Gallagher, the current union president, went into the site to look for his son, also a missing firefighter, and found him alive.

So many commanders were lost that, two days later, Giuliani had to promote 168 new officers.

At the Houston Street and Sixth Avenue station house where Evola works, ten men out of fifty were missing. A few blocks away, at West 10th Street, seven were missing. Still, the survivors kept digging. The fire department couldn't get an accurate headcount, because no one knew who had jumped on a fire truck instead of going home after the shift change, or who had not reported in because he was just too busy digging through the wreckage. Entire companies were unaccounted for—but no one knew whether they had been buried in the collapses, or whether they were simply working around the clock. It was a heroic act of insubordination. "Even if I told them to stop digging, they wouldn't," Giuliani said.

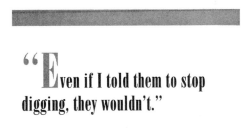

"**E**ven if I told them to stop digging, they wouldn't."

You could still see the Statue of Liberty through the smoke rising from the rubble.

There was a bronze statue, too, on a flatbed truck at 44th Street and Eighth Avenue. It shows a praying firefighter, down on one knee. It was made to honor fallen firefighters in Missouri, but the sculptor and the client who ordered it decided to donate it to New York.

For fifteen years Paula Spector walked by the Houston Street firehouse to and from work, and often she would nod to John Santore, a handsome firefighter with a handlebar mustache, who lounged in the garage. It was sort of a thing they had. She liked to think it was an unspoken, winking kind of flirtation.

The other day she was walking by the firehouse, and there he was again—on a poster. He was among those lost. Spector brought a bouquet of yellow flowers to lay on the sidewalk in front of the firehouse, but the flowers were four layers deep, and she was afraid they would get lost. She wanted these to be special, she told Evola, because they were for John Santore. Evola took the bouquet and held it like a baby. "I'll take care of them," he said and carried them inside.

Then join hand in hand, brave Americans all! By uniting we stand, by dividing we fall!

John Dickinson

The G Man

Until he retired from the FBI in August, John O'Neill, 49, was America's pit bull on terrorism. As head of the bureau's national-security operations in New York City, he oversaw investigations into the 1998 embassy bombings in Africa and the 2000 attack on the U.S.S. Cole in Yemen, both believed to be the work of groups linked to Osama bin Laden. Two weeks ago, O'Neill began a new job: chief of security at the World Trade Center.

The Yemenite government nicknamed O'Neill "Rambo." It did not use the name fondly. O'Neill didn't just request access and information from officials in Yemen; he demanded them. He insisted that his agents be allowed to carry automatic rifles for protection. Ultimately, O'Neill was barred from Yemen by U.S. Ambassador Barbara Bodine for irritating his hosts. His agents, however, were grateful for his unwavering intransigence. Said an admirer: "O'Neill has been thrown out of better places than that."

Because of his expertise, O'Neill knew exactly what terrorists could do. "A lot of these groups now have the capability and the support infrastructure in the U.S. to attack us here if they choose to," he said in 1997. Three years later, he made what could have been the defining mistake of his career: he left a briefcase full of national-security documents in a Tampa, Florida, hotel. The case was recovered unharmed, and the FBI declined to press charges. But O'Neill will not be remembered for that anomalous mistake. After the first strike on the Trade Center, it is believed he evacuated his 34th-floor office in the north tower. He made a few calls from the sidewalk—including one to his son to let him know he was unharmed and one to FBI headquarters. Then he went back in to help with the rescue effort. He has not been seen since.

A Time for Courage

The Lord our God be with us, as He was
with our fathers; may He not leave us or
forsake us; so that He may incline our
hearts to Him, to walk in all His ways . . .
that all peoples of the earth may know
that the Lord is God; there is no other.

George H. W. Bush,
41st U.S. President

Democracy Won

By Adam Mayblum

I am alive today. I am committing this to 'paper' so I never forget. SO WE NEVER FORGET.

I arrived as usual a little before 8 A.M. My office was on the eighty-seventh floor of 1 World Trade Center, a.k.a. Tower 1, a.k.a. the North Tower. Most of my associates were in by 8:30 A.M.

We were standing around, joking around, eating breakfast, checking e-mails, and getting set for the day when the first plane hit just a few stories above us. I must stress that we did not know that it was a plane. The building lurched violently and shook as if it were an earthquake. People screamed. I watched out my window as the building seemed to move ten to twenty feet in each direction. It rumbled and shook long enough for me to get my wits about myself and grab a coworker and seek shelter under a doorway. Light fixtures and parts of the ceiling collapsed. The kitchen was destroyed. We were certain that it was a bomb.

We looked out the windows. Reams of paper were flying everywhere, like a ticker tape parade.

Smoke started billowing in through the holes in the ceiling.

I looked down at the street. I could see people in Battery Park City looking up. Smoke started billowing in through the holes in the ceiling. I believe that there were thirteen of us. We did not panic. I can only assume that we thought that the worst was over. The building was standing, and we were shaken but alive.

We checked the halls. The smoke was thick and white and did not smell like I imagined smoke should smell. Not like your BBQ or your fireplace or even a bonfire. The phones were working. My wife had taken our nine-month-old for his check up. I called our nanny at home and told her to page my wife, tell her that a bomb went off, I was OK, and on my way out.

I grabbed my laptop. I took off my T-shirt and ripped it into three pieces. Soaked it in water. Gave two pieces to my friends. Tied my piece around my face to act as an air filter. And we all started moving to the staircase. One of my dearest friends said that he was staying until the police or firemen came to get him.

In the halls, there were tiny fires and sparks. The ceiling had collapsed in the men's bathroom. It was gone, along with anyone who may have been in there. We did not go in to look. We missed the staircase on the first run and had to double back. Once in the staircase, we picked up fire extinguishers, just in case.

On the eighty-fifth floor, a brave associate of mine and I headed back up to our office to drag out my partner who had stayed behind. There was no air, just white smoke. We made the rounds through the office calling his name. No response. He must have succumbed to the smoke. We left, defeated in our efforts, and made our way back to the stairwell.

We proceeded to the seventy-eighth floor where we had to change over to a different stairwell. Seventy-eight is the main junction to switch to the upper floors. I expected to see more people. There were some fifty to sixty more. Not enough. Wires and fires all over the place. Smoke, too. A brave man was fighting a fire with the emergency hose. I stopped with two friends to make sure that everyone from our office was accounted for. We ushered them and confused people into the stairwell. In retrospect, I recall seeing Harry, my head trader, doing the same several yards behind me. Although, I am only thirty-five, I have known him for over fourteen years.

I headed into the stairwell with two friends. We were moving down very orderly in Stair Case A. Very slowly. No panic. At least not overt panic. My legs could not stop shaking. My heart was pounding. Some nervous jokes and laughter. I made a crack about ruining a brand new pair of Merrells. Even still, they were right, my feet felt great. We all laughed.

We checked our cell phones. Surprisingly, there was a very good signal, but the Sprint network was jammed. I heard that the Blackberry two-way e-mail devices worked perfectly. On the phones, one out of twenty dial attempts got through. I knew I could not reach my wife so I called my parents. I told them what happened and that we were all okay and on the way down. Soon, my sister-in-law reached me. I told her we were fine and moving down. I believe that was about the sixty-fifth floor. We were bored and nervous. I called my friend Angel in San Francisco. I knew he would be watching. He was amazed I was on the phone. He told me to get out, that there was another plane on its way. I did not know what he was talking about. By now, the second plane had struck Tower 2. We were so deep into the middle of our building that we did not hear or feel anything. We had no idea what was really going on.

W e were so deep into the middle of our building that we did not hear or feel anything.

We kept making way for wounded to go down ahead of us. Not many of them, just a few. No one seemed seriously wounded. Just some cuts and scrapes. Everyone cooperated. Everyone was a hero yesterday. No questions asked. I had coworkers in another office on the seventy-seventh floor. I tried dozens of times to get them on their cell phones or office lines. It was futile. Later, I found that they were alive. One of the many miracles on a day of tragedy.

On the fifty-third floor, we came across a very heavyset man sitting on the stairs. I asked if he needed help or if he were just resting. He needed help. I knew I would have trouble carrying him because I have a very bad back. But my friend and I offered anyway. We told him he could lean on us. He hesitated; I don't know why. I asked, "Do you want to come or do you want us to send help for you?" He chose to wait for help. I told him he was on the fifty-third floor in Stairwell A and that's what I would tell the rescue workers. He said, "okay," and we left.

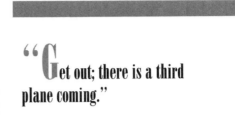

"Get out; there is a third plane coming."

On the forty-fourth floor my phone rang again. It was my parents. They were hysterical. I said, "Relax, I'm fine." My father said "Get out; there is a third plane coming." I still did not understand. I was kind of angry. What did my parents think? Like I needed some other reason to get going? I couldn't move the thousand people in front of me any faster. Yet no one inside understood what the situation really was. My parents knew.

Starting around this floor, the firemen, policemen, WTC K-9 units without the dogs, anyone with a badge, started coming up as we were heading down. I stopped a lot of them and told them about the man on 53 and my friend on 87. I later felt terrible about this. They headed up to find those people and met death instead.

On the thirty-third floor, I spoke with a man who somehow knew most of the details. He said two small planes hit the building. Now, we all started talking about which terrorist group it was. Was it an internal organization or an external one? The overwhelming but uninformed opinion was Islamic Fanatics. Regardless, we now knew that it was not a bomb and that there were potentially more planes coming. We understood.

On the third floor, the lights went out, and we heard and felt this rumbling coming towards us from above. I thought the staircase was collapsing upon itself. It was 10 A.M. now, and that was Tower 2 collapsing next door. We did not know that. Someone had a flashlight. We passed it forward and left the stairwell and headed down a dark and cramped corridor to an exit. We could not see at all. I recommended that everyone place a hand on the shoulder of the person in front of them and call out if they hit an obstacle, so others would know to avoid it. They did. It worked perfectly.

We reached another stairwell and saw a female officer emerge soaking wet and covered in soot. She said we could not go that way because it was blocked. "Go up to 4 and use the other exit," she told us. Just as we started up, she said it was OK to go down instead. There was water everywhere. I called out for hands on shoulders again, and she said that was a great idea. She stayed behind instructing people to do that. I do not know what happened to her.

We emerged into an enormous room. It was light but filled with smoke. I commented to a friend that it must be under construction. Then we realized where we were. It was the second floor. The one that overlooks the lobby. We were ushered out into the courtyard, the one where the fountain used to be. My first thought was of a TV movie I saw once about nuclear winter and fallout. I could not understand where all of the debris came from. There was at least five inches of this gray pasty dusty drywall soot on the ground as well as a thickness of it in the air. Twisted steel and wires. I heard there were bodies and body parts as well, but I did not look. It was bad enough.

We hid under the remaining overhangs and moved out to the street. We were told to keep walking towards Houston Street. The odd thing is that there were very few rescue workers around. Less than five. They all must have been trapped under the debris when Tower 2 fell. We did not know that and could not understand where all of that debris came from. It was just my friend Kern and me now. We were hugging but sad. We felt certain that most of our friends ahead of us died, and we knew no one behind us.

We came upon a post office several blocks away. We stopped and looked up. Our building, exactly where our office is (was), was engulfed in flame and smoke. A postal worker said that Tower 2 had fallen down. I looked again and sure enough it was gone. My heart was racing. We kept trying to call our families. I could not get in touch with my wife. Finally, I got through to my parents. Relieved is not the word to explain their feelings. They got through to my wife, thank God, and let her know I was alive. We sat down. A girl on a bike offered us some water. Just as she took the cap off her bottle, we heard a rumble. We looked up and our building, Tower 1 collapsed. I did not note the time, but I am told it was 10:30 A.M. We had been out less than fifteen minutes.

We were mourning our lost friends, particularly the one who stayed in the office as we were now sure that he had perished. We started walking towards Union Square. I was going to Beth Israel Medical Center to be looked at. We stopped to hear the president speaking on the radio. My phone rang. It was my wife. I think I fell to my knees crying when I heard

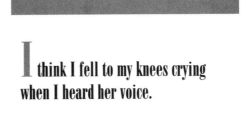

I think I fell to my knees crying when I heard her voice.

her voice. Then she told me the most incredible thing. My

partner who had stayed behind called her. He was alive and well. I guess we just lost him in the commotion. We started jumping and hugging and shouting. I told my wife that my brother had arranged for a hotel in midtown. He can be very resourceful in that way. I told her I would call her from there. My brother and I managed to get a gypsy cab to take us home to Westchester instead. I cried on my son and held my wife until I fell asleep.

As it turns out, my partner, the one who I thought had stayed behind was behind us with Harry Ramos, our head trader. This is now second-hand information. They came upon Victor, the heavyset man on the fifty-third floor. They helped him. He could barely move. My partner bravely/stupidly tested the elevator on the fifty-second floor. He rode it down to the sky lobby on 44. The doors opened, it was fine. He rode it back up and got Harry and Victor. I don't yet know if anyone else joined them. Once on 44, they made their way back into the stairwell.

Someplace around the thirty-ninth to thirty-sixth floors they felt the same rumble I felt on the third floor. It was 10 A.M. and Tower 2 was coming down. They had about thirty minutes to get out. Victor said he could no longer move. They offered to have him lean on them. He said he couldn't do it. My partner hollered at him to sit on his butt and scooch down the steps. He said he was not capable of doing it. Harry told my partner to go ahead of them. Harry had once had a heart attack and was worried about this man's heart. It was his nature to be this way. He was/is one of the kindest people I know. He would not leave a man behind. My partner went ahead and made it out. He said he was out maybe ten minutes before the building came down.

Democracy Won

This means that Harry had maybe twenty-five minutes to move Victor thirty-six floors. I guess they moved one floor every 1.5 minutes. Just a guess. This means Harry was around the twentieth floor when the building collapsed. As of now, twelve of thirteen people are accounted for. As of 6 P.M. yesterday, his wife had not heard from him. I fear that Harry is lost. However, a short while ago I heard that he may be alive. Apparently there is a web site with survivor names on it, and his name appears there. Unfortunately, Ramos is not an uncommon name in New York. Pray for him and all those like him.

With regards to the firemen heading upstairs, I realize that they were going up anyway. But, it hurts to know that I may have made them move quicker to find my friend. Rationally, I know this is not true and that I am not the responsible one. The responsible ones are in hiding somewhere on this planet. But they should know that they failed in terrorizing us. We were calm. Those men and women who went up were heroes in the face of it all. They must have known what was going on and they did their jobs. Ordinary people were heroes too.

Today the images that people around the world equate with power and democracy are gone, but "America" is not an image; it is a concept. That concept is only strengthened by our pulling together as a team. If you want to kill us, leave us alone because we will do it by ourselves. If you want to make us stronger, attack, and we unite. This is the ultimate failure of terrorism against the United States and the ultimate price we pay to be free—to decide where we want to work, what we want to eat, and when and where we want to go on vacation. The very moment the first plane was hijacked, democracy won.

One Meeting Away

By Lynette Troyer

Every single morning of a typical work week, between 8:30 and 9:00 A.M., my schedule involves traveling to the World Trade Center (WTC) via subway, often dropping by the ATM machine or stopping in one of the shops for a fast bargain, then grabbing a quick vegetable juice for breakfast and heading into yet another train station further below the WTC that takes me to Jersey City just across the Hudson River where our marketing group offices are located. Except for God's divine protection, yesterday should have been no different.

Instead of my typical commute schedule, I was picked up at home by a car service at 5 A.M. to drive two hours to Hartford, Connecticut, for a meeting I was leading. The night before, I had debated whether to go since it was such a long drive and I'd had laryngitis for four days prior, but I finally convinced myself to make the commute. At approximately 9:15 A.M. during the meeting, several people's cell phones started ringing with the news that a plane had crashed into the World Trade Center. Our first thought was that it was a small commuter plane or the like. It was when one of the men checked his Internet connection that I heard a sickening, "Oh, NO." We all rushed into a room where the television was on. We were instantly frozen: this was a tragedy unlike any other seen before.

This was a tragedy unlike any other seen before.

I cannot describe the gut-wrenching agony and disbelief I felt as we watched the two Twin Towers crumbling to the ground. I couldn't quit sobbing, as I imagined so many of my coworkers and friends potentially trapped in the wreckage, wreckage that had once been the massive WTC lobbies, parking lots, and subway stations. Our main Deloitte offices in the World Financial Center adjoin the WTC with a large walkway where many of our people are assigned to client sites. I thought of them now. *Who was in there? Did they get out? What about other friends who work down there? Oh, God, help them. Help us all,* I prayed. After calling my parents to assure them that I had indeed gone to Hartford as planned, I tried desperately to reach my coworkers, but phone lines were down or jammed, and even still (Wednesday at about 1:30 P.M.), we're unable to access voice mails or e-mails through the servers there.

Though my apartment is uptown and quite a distance from the bombing site, I knew I'd be unable to get home for some time with the bridges and tunnels closed down. I checked into the Hartford Hilton and spent the next eight hours glued to the television, waves of sobbing coming over me from time to time as reality began to seep in.

On my way home amidst literally thousands of people rushing to and fro, often bumping into each other, I remembered. It had been about one month before on a warm afternoon as I headed into the WTC subway station that I had experienced a peculiar sensation. Somehow I had felt that the building was strangely vulnerable. *Strange,* I remembered thinking to myself after having lived in New York City for two years, marveling daily at the awesome infrastructures. It's hard to fathom that those buildings are rubble now and that many of those people are still lost in the rubble, their families grieving, countless lives changed forever.

It's a strange mix of sentiments—grief at the unfathomable loss, personal gratitude for what was clearly God's divine protection, but mostly, the sentiment of a serious and renewed mission. The mission that prompted my move to this city in the first place: the CALLING that I just couldn't resist, to be LIGHT and HOPE and AUTHENTICITY in a city preoccupied with so much else, and now a city grappling with unimaginable loss.

My prayer is that I will be more BOLD than ever in articulating HOW and WHY the Gospel is relevant to our gravest sufferings and most desperate questions. Please pray for the Lord to use this tragedy for His purposes of reaching people with His love.

Pentagon 'Heroes' Knew What to Do

ARLINGTON, Va. (AP)—They believed they were in the most secure building in the strongest country in the world. Then a hijacked plane smashed into the Pentagon, their fortress. Yet they knew just what to do.

Knocked onto his back, Army Lt. Col. Victor Correa picked himself up from the floor and helped dazed colleagues out of the room. He headed for a wall of smoke down a hall littered with ceiling tiles, illuminated only by distant flames.

His big, booming voice was a natural to lead people to safety.

"I was screaming, 'Listen to me. Listen to me. Follow my voice,'" Correa recalled. "Folks started coming out."

Correa peered into the smoke, a water-soaked T-shirt pressed to his face. No one had to tell him what to do. "All of us had a different function, and I knew what mine was," he said.

All across the Pentagon, years of military training and discipline kicked in.

After an unfounded warning that a second aircraft was on its way, Correa forced open fire doors that had slammed shut. He went back in and started shouting again.

His shouting drew Carl Mahnken back to consciousness. Mahnken, a civilian in the army public affairs office, got up from the rubble-strewn floor and followed the voices through the smoke. Outside, he saw medics assisting the wounded. He ran over to help.

"You knew what to do, you ripped pants open, you took shoes off, you learned to help people with their shock, to get the blood flowing," said Mahnken, an Army reservist trained in first aid.

It was not until hours later, in the evening, that a firefighter told Mahnken about the golf-ball-size bump protruding from his crown. That was when he remembered his computer terminal flying toward his head, hours earlier.

"He gave me an ice pack," he said. "I hadn't noticed."

Army Sgt. Maj. Tony Rose heard cries for help from behind a mountain of debris inside one room and set up a tunnel-digging team, working on rotation. One particularly hefty Navy Seal propped up the sagging ceiling.

One particularly hefty Navy Seal propped up the sagging ceiling.

"I forget his name," Rose said. "We just called him 'Big John.'"

They had helped seven people out through the impromptu tunnel when a wall buckled. They got out before it collapsed.

There was a call for volunteers in another area.

"There were some walking wounded, but everyone who could turned back," Rose said. "We had no maps, no flashlights, just wet T-shirts."

Some refused even to talk about themselves, insisting on recounting the heroism they witnessed. Lt. Col. Sean Kelly singled out Army colleague Capt. Darrell Oliver.

After Kelly and Oliver lifted a desk off a secretary, Oliver hoisted her onto his back and carried her out. Then he returned for a hearing impaired janitor who was sobbing in fear. "He calmed him down, he carried him out over the partitions, over the furniture," Kelly said.

Kelly also noted National Guard Lt. Col. Larry Dudney, hacking from smoke inhalation as he lifted furniture off of his colleagues.

Military training was key to the disciplined response.

Each man said military training was key to the disciplined response—although each hastened to note that the civilians were also cool and resourceful.

"The thing with the military," Kelly said, "is that you ask for one volunteer, you get fifty—you're trained for crisis."

Rose marveled as he recalled shouting orders at generals among the volunteers bagging body parts around the wreckage.

"I sort of became the old sergeant major out there," he said. "People, regardless of rank, fell in and did what was needed."

Constantly on the rescuers' minds is the thought about what was left undone: 188 people believed dead from the plane and the Defense Department headquarters.

"I knew I had to leave when [the smoke] got worse. I think I did the right thing," Correa said. "There are questions I'll have to live with for the rest of my life."

Some answers have already come: "I've been approached by several folks who said, 'That was the voice I heard.'"

Reprinted with Permission of the Associated Press.

In a Dark Time, Light

In Manhattan, where "good" is just the name of a restaurant in Greenwich Village and "evil" is what we call the prices at the new Chanel store in SoHo, the concept of miracles seemed a little hokey until last week. A pointy-head at one of the city's universities might have said the idea of the miraculous is an old metaphor that needs demystifying. But there's nothing metaphorical about what happened to Genelle Guzman, 31, an office manager who worked on the sixty-fourth floor of Tower One. She called her boyfriend, Roger McMillan, just after the blast and told him she was waiting at her desk, as instructed over the loudspeaker.

McMillan, 38, a pressman for a direct-mail company, could see the explosions from his workplace, and told her to get out and meet him in front of Century 21, a discount fashion emporium across from the World Trade Center.

He ran and walked twenty blocks, past bloody survivors and jet parts, until he saw the street in front of the store. It was a mountain of detritus. He searched in vain, then called his voice mail. Guzman had left a message saying once again she was staying put, as instructed. "I lost all hope when I heard that," he says.

What he didn't know was that Guzman had started down the stairs when word came to evacuate. At floor 13, the building collapsed, and Guzman's head was caught between two pillars. She lay in fear and agony for hours. She felt a man trapped near her and pushed next to him for comfort. She heard him cry out twice; eventually, he fell silent. She repeatedly asked God, "Please give me a second chance at life." There was only darkness and dust. So she said another prayer: "Please just give me this one miracle." And a man appeared above her, a saint named Paul, who lifted her from the rubble. Twenty-six hours had passed.

Now at Bellevue Hospital, Guzman is one of just five victims rescued from the Trade Center after Tuesday. Her head is swollen, and her legs required surgery, but doctors expect full recovery. Guzman and McMillan, Trinidadian immigrants who live in Brooklyn, plan many changes. "Before, we went to church on a couple of occasions," says McMillan. "It's something you put off. But Genelle already stated in the hospital bed that this is her calling to God." The two plan to marry.

A Note to Friends and Family

By Cary Sheih

Now that I can begin to think clearly again, I would like to take the time to thank each and every one of you for your concern for my well being. It was a very close call, and I am grateful to be alive.

As you probably all know by now, I narrowly escaped from the World Trade Center attack this past Tuesday, unlike the thousands who are still trapped beneath the rubble. At 8:48 A.M. on Tuesday morning, I was reading my e-mail like I do every morning. I had just gotten off the phone with a traffic engineer at the Port Authority regarding a file that I had transmitted to him on the previous day. As I was finishing off my usual peanut butter and jelly sandwich, I heard a loud explosion, which was immediately followed by tremendous building sways and vibrations. As I was thrown out of my chair, I immediately thought that this was an earthquake, but still thinking rationally, I thought that it was abnormal since there are no earthquakes in New York City, especially of this magnitude. I remember thinking that the building felt like it was going to collapse from this initial explosion.

> The building felt like it was going to collapse from this initial explosion.

As I picked myself up and ran to the emergency staircase located in the core of the huge building, I saw through the east facing windows debris and fireballs falling from the top of the building. The building had stabilized by the time I reached the stairwell, and evacuation had commenced quickly but calmly. Not knowing the gravity of what was happening above us, people had started pouring into the stairwell from the hallways of the different floors. I saw a co-worker from my floor (seventy-second), and we held and consoled each other.

There were no public announcements in the stairwell, but the evacuation seemed to be going smoothly; there were no more explosions as far as we could tell, no smoke coming up the stairwell, and the building had stopped swaying. We all felt like we were out of imminent danger. As we started to make it down the stairwell, people started chatting and gathering their composure. I heard some people who had been there in '93 telling others that this was a piece of cake since the stairwell was dark and full of smoke in '93. Others were joking about how Mr. Silverstein, who had just recently taken control of the complex, must be fuming at what was happening.

A few moments passed, and people began to receive messages over their pagers that a 767 had accidentally hit our building. There was no mention of a terrorist attack, and at no time was there any panic. Mobile phones were completely out in the core of the building due to its immenseness and the large distance from the core of the building to the exterior, where signals were usually stronger. There was no smoke at all in the stairwell, but there was a peculiar smell, which I later remembered as smelling like it does when one boards an aircraft. I later found out that this was jet fuel.

Soon we heard shouts from the people above us to keep to the right. I started seeing blind people, those with difficulty moving, asthmatics, and injured people filing down to our left. People were burned so badly that I won't go into detail. People kept filing down orderly and calmly, but stunned.

Somewhere around the thirtieth or fortieth floor, we passed the first firefighters coming up the stairs. They reassured people that we were safe and that we would all get out fine. By this point, they were already absolutely breathless, but still pushing upward, slowly and unyieldingly, one step at a time. I could only imagine how tired they were, carrying their axes, hoses, and heavy outfits and climbing up all those stairs. Young men started offering to carry up the firefighters' gear for a few flights, but they all refused. EACH and EVERY ONE of them. As I relive this moment over and over in my mind, I can't help but think that these courageous firefighters already knew in their minds that they would not make it out of the building alive and that they didn't want to endanger any more civilians and prevent one person from making it to safety on the ground.

We continued down the stairwell, slowly and at times completely stalled. The smell of jet fuel had gotten so unbearable that people began covering their mouths and noses with anything that they could find—ties, shirts, handkerchiefs. Every few floors, emergency crew were passing out water and sodas from the vending machines that they had split open from the hallways. I had no idea how much time had passed as I didn't have my mobile phone with me. Around the twentieth or fifteenth floor, the emergency crew began diverting the people in our stairwell to a different stairwell. They led us out of our stairwell, across the hallway where I saw exhausted firefighters and emergency crew sitting on the floor trying to catch their breath. I began to think *Why? What's going on?* This whole operation looked very confusing.

Nobody was giving us any indication as to what was going on. The wait in the hallway to get to the other staircase was excruciatingly long, as we had to wait and merge with the people who were coming down the staircase into which we were filing. Why had they diverted us? As we started to get down to the lower floors, water started to pour down from behind us. I figured that a water pipe had burst or that it was water coming down from the rescue on the higher floors.

I was not ready for this apocalyptic scene.

At this moment for the first time since the initial explosion, a sense of panic began to grip me. Only floor 7, then 6. A few more to go, and I would be free. I couldn't wait. It didn't matter that the water was ankle deep. I was a few floors from the ground. Floor 4. Then all of a sudden, a loud boom, and the building began to shake unbearably again. People started falling down the stairwell as smoke started to rise from the bottom. The emergency lights flickered and then went out. The building was still shaking, and I could hear the steel buckling. Rescuers below us shouted for us to go back up the stairs. At this moment, I was choking and shaking tremendously. I managed to climb back up to the sixth or seventh floor and opened the door to that floor. The water had already risen to my ankles, and the floor was completely dark. A fireman led us with his flashlight to another staircase by the voices of another fireman who was guiding him through the darkness. We finally made it across that floor to the other stairwell where we were greeted by the other fireman and told to hold on. The look on that fireman's face said it all. He said something under his breath to our fireman indicating the severity of the situation.

In hindsight, with the image of the firemen communicating to each other, I believe that the fireman had whispered to the other one that Building Two had collapsed.

After a few minutes of huddling by the stairwell on the sixth floor, we were given the green light to run for our lives. I made it down six flights with a few other people and came out onto the mezzanine level of our building. I don't know what I was expecting to see when I got out of the stairwell, but I was not ready for this apocalyptic scene. It was completely covered in white dust and smoke. My initial reaction was that I couldn't believe that one plane, albeit a 767, eighty floors above our head caused all this damage on the ground floor—inside. I covered my head and ran towards the huge opening in the north side of the building through which we were being evacuated.

As I approached this threshold, the firefighters yelled to us to get over to the wall of the building quickly. Debris was still raining from all sides of the building. We could see the other firefighters who were outside standing underneath the cantilevered parts of the black Immigration building (4 and/or 5 WTC). At their cue, we ran from our building to the outside world and back underneath the Immigration building. I was completely disoriented, coughing, and looking at the strange new landscape at the WTC plaza—burning trees, wreckage, fireballs and dust, nothing short of a nuclear winter. I climbed over huge pieces of steel wreckage and made my way through to the skybridge leading to 7 WTC (the third building to collapse). From there, I descended the escalators down to the street level onto Vesey Street and trotted to safety onto Church Street. I immediately looked back and saw the charred remains of the upper floors of my building. Smoke filled the sky, and I began to have this eerie feeling that WTC 2 was not there. I couldn't be sure because of all the smoke that was billowing from my building blowing eastward. As I was trying to find WTC 2, I saw the unthinkable happen in front of my eyes. WTC 1 began to disintegrate from where it was burning. I turned around and ran.

I later learned that another 767 had hit WTC 2 around the floors where I sit in my building. WTC 2 had collapsed when we were still inside my building on the fourth floor when it began to shake for a second time. I later learned that I had been spared from the sight of people falling from the higher floors. I am grateful to be alive and uninjured and to be able to share this life-changing experience with you. And, I am so grateful for the courage of the firefighters and police officers who gave up their lives to help us down the burning tower.

World Champion Swimmer Ian Thorpe

A forgotten camera might have saved Australian swimming star Ian Thorpe from being at the World Trade Center when it was attacked by terrorists. He was on a promotional visit to New York and was planning a trip to the buildings moments before he heard about the terrorist attack on the first tower. Frank Turner, one of Thorpe's managers, said if the attack had occurred twenty minutes later, the Olympic and world champion would have been on the viewing deck at the top of one of the towers. He said Thorpe awoke early Tuesday and walked past the World Trade Center. He returned to his hotel for his camera and headed back to the tower to take some photos. Just as he was about to leave his room, he turned on the TV and saw that the first tower had been attacked.

One Can of Coffee

After hearing the reports on television that no one could get down to the "Ground Zero" epicenter of the World Trade Center tragedy, I had reserved a spot on the couch for my third night in a row of watching television and waiting, wishing I could "do more". On air, a local news reporter invited a teenage volunteer to say what supplies were needed down at the scene, and he responded, "the firefighters need coffee." So I looked at my friend who was similarly camped on the couch next to me, and we both said, "we can get coffee."

We headed out to the corner grocery store. Our intended single can of coffee became four cans....in addition to three pizza pies and 3 gallon jugs of water from a local pizzeria, which we shepherded into a taxi to head down to Chelsea Piers, where the coffee was needed. The "drop-off" area was actually the distribution point for community stores to donate goods - supplies of paper towels, cloth towels, packs of bottled water, vast quantities of Chewy Granola bars and work gloves. Individuals also brought supplies - six packs of soda; personal clothing such as t-shirts, pants, and boxer shorts for the rescue workers; even sandwiches which were individually wrapped in lunch bags, made by an elderly woman for 'the boys'. One young boy came over with his parents, struggling under the weight of a gallon cranberry juice bottle, label half peeled off, which he proudly said he had filled with water for the "policemen who fight fires".

Without being told what to do, everyone fell into line, the "pass the bucket" variety in which you grab from your right and pass to your left, to get everything off the trucks and into piles on the pier. One by one, NYC Police harbor patrol boats motored up to the pier to be loaded with supplies to be brought down to the firemen and policemen working at the site. Food was needed, so with three big tins of heated ziti in hand, I joined the five other volunteers carrying supplies onboard the Police Shuttle Boat...only when I was handed a filtered mask did I fully realize where I was headed.

It was warm out, even on the river while wearing shorts and a t-shirt; the lights of Manhattan's buildings shone clear into the night. Any other night it would have been gorgeous – any other night the southern end of the New York City skyline wouldn't have had a giant cloud of white smoke billowing up into darkness. As we headed into the financial center marina, the air quality got worse and I had full view of the destruction. The last time I had been on that exact dock was a few years ago for a dinner cruise with a client. That evening, the windows glistened, the side of the buildings gleamed in the sun, and the colorful flags along the harbor flapped proudly in the wind.

Now, the dull, burnt brown-red color flags were still, at half mast. The buildings were covered in white-gray ash. Paperwork of those who used to work so far above lay strewn all over the pier. Mangled corners of buildings near the Towers hung loosely, a banana peel of window frames and twisted metal. The World Financial Center glass atrium, the

Winter Garden, had been devastated; only a ghostly metal frame remained. The only lights reflected on the few remaining atrium windows came not from the internal lights spotlighting decorative palm trees as in the past, but the eerie refraction from the bright worklights being used at the rescuers' site. With ash on everything, buildings cut and windows blown out, it looked very much like a science fiction cartoon picture, or an unfinished movie set painted in a single matte color without texture delineation...it was unreal.

We carried the supplies off the boat and piled them in the principle loading area by the pier. In anticipation of the impending storm, everything had been moved under the building ledges where restaurant outdoor café tables and chairs once were arranged. Piles of clothing and towels, medical supplies, work supplies like shovels and pick axes, and food lay arranged in their proper area to be taken as needed to the "up front" area. Clutching my pans of ziti, I sloshed through the mud puddles, and navigated around the fire hoses that lay all over the ground, through what was once the World Financial Center complex towards the worker's area. Messages written in the ash that covered the windows bolstered the spirit: "Let's Show the World", "America Stand Strong", "For Bobby" and "Thank You". I walked through the building and emerged on the plaza side, facing what were once the World Trade Center towers, and stopped short.

To my left, the mass of twisted steel, heaps of concrete and huge polished metal sidings of Atlas proportions seemed never-ending. Firemen were climbing all over the mounds of rubble, passing buckets of rock, dirt and cement blocks one-by-one. The sheer volume of rescuers and the horribly immense pile of material to be cleared was unimaginable. Just when you might have thought you were at a construction site, or a junkyard, you'd find a shoe. Just lying there.

After passing out food briefly, I worked the rest of the evening and into the morning reorganizing the rescuer's supplies inside what was once the One Financial Center lobby, placing gloves, masks, towels, socks, batteries, long sleeve shirts and sundry other items in the respective piles I assigned. The escalators were still and dirt was everywhere, but the roof was solid...and would provide needed protection from the expected rain.

The rescue volunteers humbled me. When I asked one fireman if he wanted to lie down to rest, he pointed at a picture of his wife and daughter, which was taped to his arm. "Every time I get tired, I think of them, and I have the energy I need," he said. A number of policemen there were "off-duty" - the Force didn't want them to risk injury, so they weren't allowed to work at Ground Zero while on the job. On their off hours, however, they can do as they like...and after working 12-16 hour "official" shifts, they came back at Ground Zero, ready to help. One policeman made a compromise with his terrified wife that he'd call her every hour to tell her that he's ok.

The rain came pounding down, and still the rescuers stayed out there. We ran out of rain gear, and I hated to tell them we didn't have anything to keep them dry. We even ran out of garbage bags for a while from which they had been fashioning slickers. Rather than get mad, they simply shrugged and said, "that's ok, thanks for your help." We ran out of long sleeve shirts, and though they must have been freezing in their unprotected wet clothing, when I told them that we were still waiting for shirts from the stockpile, they said, "ok, thank you for looking." I don't know any of their names, because they all referred to each other as 'Brother'. They helped me to carry my carts of clothing from the supply piles over the fire hoses, and were incredibly gentle and polite. They continually asked me if I had eaten anything, and even took off their coats and offered them to me in case I was cold. I couldn't believe with everything they were doing, they took the time to check on me.

"Hey, Columbia," shouted one volunteer covered in dirt, sweat and ashes, seeing the name of my alma mater on my t-shirt. "I'm class of '68, what about you?" What a place to get connected, to remember that while "Six Degrees of Separation" may be a socially acceptable "rule", the WTC disaster seemed have reduced our world to "two degrees of connection." By the time my new friend finally went home, he had slept four hours out of the 124 he had been working at the site.

I had no idea what kind of wonderful, caring people we have protecting our city. Like many New Yorkers, I thought of firefighters and police as part of New York's fabric, but never really paid attention to them unless I needed them or thought I might get a parking ticket. Never again will I fail to notice these heroes. In the shadows of hell, within the twisted remains of my hometown's broken skyline, they fight to find survivors. They fight when there is no hope because they believe there must be hope. They will not give up. They just keep going out to Ground Zero. They nap for a few minutes, and then they're right back on the pile. It was a privilege for me to help out, even just for a little while, to "do more". They were there when I arrived in the evening and they remained after I left in the morning...they will not leave...and they're simply remarkable.

Panic, Anxiety Followed Plane's Impact at Pentagon

By Lisa Burgess

During the Cold War, everyone who worked in the Pentagon called the center courtyard of the Pentagon "Ground Zero" — a sick joke based on the rumor that the Soviet Union based all its nuclear missile coordinates on the lunch stand at the heart of the building.

On Tuesday, long after the joke had supposedly died, Ground Zero came true.

More than the usual number of people were in the Pentagon's courtyard Tuesday at 9:40 A.M. because the weather was gorgeous. I was inside, walking down an inside corridor toward the Metro, trying to dodge two janitors moving their clumsy gray trash bin and a pair of fast-moving Army officers rolling up on my heels. A tremendous vibration and boom, followed quickly by a second, less-intense boom, rattled the gallery of former Defense Secretaries whose portraits hang in the corridor. Both janitors tumbled to the floor, curling and rolling to avoid being hit by the trash cart. The soldiers and I hit the wall.

The soldiers and I hit the wall.

"What was that?" one of the soldiers gasped.

We all turned to look out the floor-to-ceiling plate glass window and saw a rolling fireball across the courtyard. Outside, people were fleeing a curtain of smoke dropping from the rooftop toward the snack shack at the courtyard's center. I knew people were screaming because I could see their mouths open, but I couldn't hear them. There was no doubt we'd been hit, and that it was somehow connected to what had just happened to the World Trade Center in New York.

The building's evacuation happened very fast. The Pentagon's 20,000 civilians and service members wore uniformly puzzled and concerned expressions as they filled the halls, but they were well-drilled, and the building was empty in a matter of minutes. Then, confusion.

About 150 people ended up in the courtyard, including medical personnel from the on-site clinic and the Pentagon Athletic Club, as well as a good number of security workers.

A trickle of wounded began staggering out of the doors of the damaged section. Those less hurt were half-dragging, half-carrying others. All the victims were choking and coughing because the fire was growing stronger by the minute. The smoke rising above the building blotted out the sun.

At least two people were badly burned, one of whom literally had his clothing burned off—blinded, unrecognizable, holding his blackened and melted arms in front of himself like a Frankenstein parody as medics tried desperately to find a vein to start an IV.

I later saw one brown loafer and the rags of his charred BVDs beneath the spot where he sat. An older civilian manager came out under his own power. Blood was running down his face and staining his T-shirt. His dress shirt and shoes were gone. He was dazed and upset, but calm—a Vietnam-era Marine—and he said. "My wife is in there."

He said he had been in the common area of his office when the explosion happened, along with a group of women who were standing by the Xerox machine. The Xerox exploded and so did they, he said. I tried to get him to sit, but just as he was lowering himself to a bench, three Pentagon security officers, who had walkie-talkies, began to shout, "There's another hijacked plane inbound! It's headed this way, and we have five minutes to impact!" The mood in the yard had been intense but purposeful. Now it turned to panic. No one knew where to go. Where was safety?

The three most-wounded were lifted onto orange utility trucks and driven back into the building, away from the fire. Medics ran alongside, worked grimly to hold pressure bandages in place as the carts careened for the ground-level tunnels that mark each corner of the courtyard.

Everyone else headed for the walls as the security screamed out a countdown of the estimated time to impact. We reached the tunnel entrance just in time to be told "false alarm." Back the group went to the lawn, where medical supplies had been abandoned in drifts alongside bloody, charred clothes.

No sooner were the triage teams reassembled than the alarm came: the plane was inbound. This was a no-kidder. Everyone had to go *now*. Again, the group scrambled.

I ended up in a hallway with an Army officer and an Air Force officer—both paramedics—and a woman in civilian clothing who said she was a veterinarian. Before this little team evacuated the yard, we had stuffed every medical box and bag of supplies we could grab on the lawn onto an orange motor cart—the ones the maintenance guys zoom around in at the Pentagon because the place is so big.

Minutes passed. No sound of low engines. No crash. The four of us decided to use the cart to try to get as close as we could to the crash site. Maybe we could get some more people out of the fire. The courtyard was now empty except for a few firefighters as we headed for the smoke, the officers in front and the other woman and myself hanging off the back.

One of the firefighters tossed us two full fire extinguishers as we entered the building. He pointed up. "Watch out for the smoke. It's really bad up there."

But in the end, the smoke got us. We tried three different ways to get anywhere near the center of the crash, but without oxygen masks, the smoke was just too thick. We had to turn back without seeing a soul. All through that morning, volunteers trickled back into the courtyard until there were more than 100 people. A two-star general officer, a surgeon, arranged triage teams.

"If victims aren't breathing well, don't bother to insert plastic tubes down their throat, or intubate," the surgeon told the "red," or critical, team. "The smoke will have swollen their breathing passages shut. Go straight for a tracheotomy," he said. "But don't cut into anyone's throat unless you know what you're doing."

No one laughed, because he wasn't joking. Then we waited. The smoke got worse, and the crowd began coughing, but no one left. Two men took an ax to the soda machines in the snack bars, and the cold drinks were passed, with firefighters getting priority. The used cans and bottles were filled with a hose and refilled again and again by self-appointed teams. Still we waited. Not a single person had emerged since the initial trickle of victims. Finally, at 3 P.M., firefighters declared the center courtyard as the morgue, and the volunteers were sent out to the main medical staging area, where the plane had crashed. Hundreds of doctors, nurses, Red Cross volunteers, and dozens of medical teams had assembled an instant village of triage stations on the side where the aircraft had hit, a prudent distance from the carnage.

But not a single medical team was working. The white bedding on the cots was pristine. The IV bags hung in neat rows. Boxes and crates and cartons of medical supplies were stacked and opened. But there was no one to work on. There hadn't been since the initial blast, a doctor said, his eyes creasing with frustration and the fatigue of a long and fruitless wait. The silence, except for the constant sound of helicopters and roar of water from the firefighter's hoses, was deafening. Saddest of all was the row upon row of empty stretchers that lay out, ready to ferry someone to safety.

> Saddest of all was the row upon row of empty stretchers that lay out.

But there was no one to carry.

Later that night—much later—the neat rows of stretchers were replaced by neat rows of body bags. The fire was just too hot. No one could get through to the place where we all knew people lay dead.

The Stars and Stripes newspaper is the trademark of the Stars and Stripes and is reproduced with permission from European and Pacific Stars and Strips, a Department of Defense publication.

A Promise Kept Brings Joy in Midst of Sorrow

By Steve Lopez

NEW YORK – From the pews of Brooklyn's St. James Lutheran Church came the whispers.

"Is Rudy really coming?" a boy asked his mother.

"I don't know if he can make it. The mayor is very busy."

Busy enough that everyone would have forgiven Mayor Rudolph W. Giuliani if he had skipped the wedding Sunday afternoon. Almost from the moment of the attack on New York, Giuliani has been the tireless, unwavering voice of comfort and resolve, a chaplain, friend and field general.

But several weeks ago, at a funeral for a fallen firefighter, he had promised to walk the fireman's sister down the aisle. Diane Gorumba had also lost her father and grandfather to natural causes over the past year, and she and her mother, Gail, were flattered by the mayor's promise to stand in.

Nearly 200 people applauded at the sight of him.

Those who couldn't squeeze into St. James lined up Sunday on Gerritsen Avenue on the chance of spotting Giuliani. Gerritsen Beach is a neighborhood of corner grocery stores and chats on porches. It's a neighborhood of cops, sanitation workers and firefighters. More than two dozen of the firefighters missing and presumed dead at the World Trade Center are from here, where salt air blows in across the marshes, and sons and daughters follow their fathers into precinct houses and ladder companies.

"I am going to take time out to go to a wedding," Mayor Giuliani had said earlier on Sunday, mentioning how Gail Gorumba had persevered in the face of tragedy, having lost three loved ones in so short a span.

"I have thought many times about Mrs. Gorumba—she allows the pain to happen, and then she focuses on the good things in life," he said.

At ten minutes to three, the groom, police officer Michael Ferrito, took his place at the altar.

Five minutes later, the cheers on the street could be heard inside the church.

Rudy had arrived.

He was secreted in through a back door, then walked past me on his way to join the bridal party on the front steps of the church. I followed him to the vestibule and watched.

From across the street and as far down the block as Poppa's Delicatessen, nearly 200 people applauded at the sight of him. Three generations called his name, whistled and waved American flags.

The man they cheered—a man with well-publicized personal problems and an ongoing battle against cancer—wasn't just standing up for Diane Gorumba. He had been standing up for the entire city, expressing its grief and promising its survival.

That's his job, of course, and he had always acted as if he were camp counselor to 8 million citizens, many of whom got stuck in his craw. But he had never done it with such unifying grace.

"Clear the aisles," ushers ordered as the congregation moved toward the vestibule with cameras, trying to capture this moment of generosity and hope, the mayor waving to the crowd.

Giuliani descended the steps to greet Gail and Diane Gorumba, and then stood in place like a soldier. It seemed as though he had told himself to do nothing that would upstage Diane Gorumba. It wasn't his fault that when the wedding march began, and Giuliani led the bride into the church, applause erupted.

The mayor smiled broadly as he marched the bride up the aisle, then he shrank away and took a seat. An early exit would have required no explanation, but the mayor stayed for the entire ceremony, as if savoring this respite from one of the worst acts of war in the history of man.

Giuliani will be ceremonial pallbearer for more than 5,000 people before this is over. He was here on a promise, and he was here to drive home the point he had made earlier:

The suffering will not end any time soon, nor will the war. But life goes on.

When Diane and Michael were pronounced husband and wife, the mayor took his place in the greeting line outside the church and shook the hand of every last parishioner. By then, the crowd on the street had grown to nearly 300.

"Four more years," shouted one man. Giuliani is nearing the end of his second and final term as mayor.

Dozens wore NYFD shirts and hats, and one fireman told me 28 of the estimated 300 who are unaccounted for lived in Gerritsen Beach. Another 35 are from nearby Marine Park.

Kerri Orloff, fourteen, Katelyn Blundell, thirteen, and Kaitlyn Hardy, also thirteen, waved a "Thanks Rudy" sign in the middle of Gerritsen Avenue. The girls have been assembling care packages for rescue workers, and Kerri's dad is a lieutenant in Engine Company 201, which lost four firefighters at the World Trade Center.

Robert Hommel, a cop shot in the line of duty two years ago, was there with his three children and wife, Tara, who waved a flag.

A Promise Kept Brings Joy in Midst of Sorrow

"It was phenomenal that he came," said bridesmaid Angela Thomas, sister of the groom. Behind her, a woman shouted, "God bless you, Rudy."

I sat down under a shade tree next to Doris Mendez, and we took in the scene together. Almost parenthetically, she told me her son, Charles, is among the missing firemen.

"She had nobody to walk her down the aisle," Doris Mendez said as the bride got into a white limousine with her new husband. "That's a great thing the mayor did. To give us something happy to come and see in the midst of all this tragedy."

2001 Los Angeles Times, reprinted by permission.

Built on the Truth

By Scott Fehrenbacher

My job requires frequent air travel. But the experience I had at Dulles airport at 9:30 Tuesday morning on September 11 was unlike any other I have ever had.

As my wife, Joni, dropped me off at the Dulles departure area, I was making a mental note that Tuesday mornings were especially peaceful and quiet at Dulles. There were no lines at check-in or at security. While I was on the way to my boarding gate, my thoughts of my business trip were quickly interrupted by the buzzing of my pager. My wife informed me that an airplane of some kind had flown into the World Trade Center. My first response was to track down my managing editor and channel editors to coordinate coverage of the "accident" and provide a means for our audience to pray online for the victims.

Seated at my boarding gate, I made phone calls to my editors. I was seated near the adjoining gate. An American Airlines plane bound for Los Angeles was boarding at that gate a few minutes ahead of the time my plane boarded. The gate agent making loud boarding announcements was annoying to me. Finally, the plane next to me was boarded and the area was quiet. Not long afterward, the gate agent for my flight invited us to board. Just then, I overheard that someone saw on the CNN airport TV that a second plane—a commercial 767—had also flown into the World Trade Center. I realized that a major terrorist act was taking place, and a tragic story was developing.

Once I made it to my seat on the plane I kept making my calls. I called my brother on the West Coast to tell him that I was not in New York and to tell my mother so neither of them would worry about the breaking news. I told him I was safe on a flight at Dulles. As more passengers boarded, there was an increasingly uneasy feeling as everyone around me was talking about the two apparent commercial jet hijackings. I thought to myself, "Thank the Lord I'm not in Boston where those planes came from."

As I was leaving a lengthy message with our news editor, a passenger grabbed his luggage and left the plane. He actually stopped next to me, looked at me, and said, "Why are you still on this plane?" He walked off the plane and back into the terminal. Three others followed him. While I was considering what had just happened, the flight attendant shut the door, ending any thought I had of deboarding.

Our plane taxied out to the runway. A man next to me said, "This sounds callous, but I hope these plane crashes don't hurt the market any more." We talked about the markets and his worry over the economy.

Once on the runway, the pilot interrupted the passengers and said, "Ladies and gentlemen, I don't know how to say this, but due to ongoing terrorist attacks I have been instructed to return to the gate. Once we get to the gate, you are instructed to leave the plane and take all luggage with you." There was a stunned silence.

Once out of the jetway I stopped to make a phone call at the adjacent gate, where I had been seated earlier. I immediately noticed a group of American Airlines flight attendants that were there. They were hugging each other and crying hysterically. I thought that they must have heard about the American plane hijacked from Boston and gave it no more thought. My cell calls would not go through any longer. I decided I had better get a taxi and get back to my office.

On my way, I saw an airport TV that showed the Pentagon with smoke billowing out of it. I was horrified. I realized this was bigger than I thought. I hailed a taxi. The cab driver happened to be Arabic and wore a bright red turban. As I brought him my bags, I could see panic in his eyes. He lifted his hands and said, "A terrible thing . . . a terrible thing happened today." I agreed. I told him we needed to pray.

He was obviously fearful of hostile reaction to him because he was Arabic. When he dropped me off at my office, I told him I would pray for him and told him to be careful. He said, "Oh, I'm going home now. It won't be safe for me today."

Safely back in my office I first heard the news. American Airlines was missing a plane and it was feared that its flight 77—departing Dulles just after 9 a.m., en route to Los Angeles—was the hijacked flight that crashed into the Pentagon. I was shocked. I realized that less than an hour earlier, I had been one gate away from a plane of people who were on their way to their deaths, murdered by terrorists. I realized that I had been sitting among the passengers of American Airlines flight 77, and most likely even among the hijackers themselves.

I stopped and thanked God for his grace. I prayed for comfort for the families of the victims who, one hour earlier, had shared gate space with me and were thinking about the business day ahead, just as I was.

I then called my wife in disbelief. I prayed with my wife and children hours later when I arrived at home, and life's fragility was more real to me than ever before.

How do we respond to this horrific tragedy? America has historically responded to crises with prayer. We must do this again. While politicians often use Scripture only when it is advantageous to them, I was very pleased to see President Bush call the country to prayer and use Psalm 23 to comfort American families. America's foundation is secure because America's foundation is built on the truth of Jesus Christ. There its future must remain for the sake of our country and our families.

It's Okay Honey

By Mary Czekalski

I work at a school, as a Health Aid. I received a call from a concerned parent on September 11, shortly after we had all heard the terrible news from New York. She was calling to check if the school was allowing the children to see TV, or if we were carrying on with business as usual. I told her that although the superintendent had made a statement regarding the current situation, no TV's were allowed to be on in the classrooms, and yes, school was running normally.

She started to cry, and said she was so glad that the children were being sheltered from the horror of the unfolding events. She then went on to tell me that she had a little sister who works at the Pentagon. Naturally, the family was frantic. The woman told me that this was the second tragedy in their lives, as their mom had recently passed away.

The woman then went on to say that the little sister had managed to get an e-mail through to her shortly after the Pentagon building was hit. . . . apparently the little sister was to be in that building at 8 A.M. for a meeting, but overslept. She said that in her sleep she heard her mother's voice saying "it's OK honey, go back to sleep". When the little sister awoke a short time later, and turned on the radio, she had heard of the horrible news.

It seems that there are guardian angels after all.

'Is That Thunder?'

By Tony Carnes

T hirty years ago, just as the World Trade Center's two
towers were going up, nearby Primitive Christian
Church went down in flames. College student Marcos
Rivera came running back to his church to find a gutted
hollow. Now, like much of the New York church, Primitive
has rebuilt and is flourishing. Other church leaders describe
Primitive as a place where good teaching and the grace of
God have built a people with a character that can stand hard
times. It was tested Tuesday morning by the nuclear-like
explosion that flew over the neighborhood.

Rivera, now pastor of his church, was sipping his coffee
Tuesday morning. He had just picked it up at the Egyptian
diner on the corner. On his way to the church, he glanced
over his right shoulder at the towers as he does every
morning. "In the neighborhood everyone seems to do this,"
Rivera says. "We grew up with them being built and as part
of our lives."

Tuesday seemed another normal day of shuffling and reshuffling the church's schedule.

Across the street, the Rev. Nelson Santiago was splashing some water on his face at the kitchen sink, which has a window framing the towers. As usual, his mind was checking out his to-do list for the day. He didn't notice the fires on Tower One.

His secretary came into the church, saying, "Pastor, the trade tower is on fire." Rivera wondered if she was joking.

"No!" he responded.

"Yes, Pastor, come out."

Santiago and his wife Angela had finally noticed the burning tower outside their window, but they were not worried.

Closer to the towers, the feelings were rising. The High School for Leaders and Public Service stands pretty close to the towers. A smoky odor was beginning to permeate the school. Pastor Rivera's son Matthew, 15, smelled an odor like burning ink. His friend Phillip Santiago, 14, was on the next floor down, the 10th. His room had windows, but he too dismissed the smell. He thought that the papers flying around outside were another prank of a rival high school next door. He quickly returned his focus to the English class. He didn't want the students at the other high school think that they could distract him.

Then the second plane hit. In a flicker of a moment the situation turned into a vital Job-like test.

On Phillip's floor, the windows "rippled like water," one witness recalled. As the building shook, a teacher downstairs started screaming, "A bomb! A bomb!"

Phillip admits he was terrified. When the teacher told the students to continue their work, he thought, "Forget that!" The girls started to cry; the guys were furious.

Matthew immediately started packing his Timberline bag. Turning to his best friend Larry Pitta, he yelled, "I want to get out!"

Back at Primitive Christian, Rivera ran out of the church. "There was a roar of weeping when I got outside," Rivera said. "I started yelling, 'Oh God, have mercy! Protect us!'" Pacing, Rivera was thinking about his son and the other children of the church. Finally, he decided to stay for his people. "I got a hold of myself. I had always told my son to come home in such event and not be spectator. I was pretty sure he would do that."

Santiago and his wife were already on their way to the school but got blocked by police vehicles strewn like pebbles. They turned to each other. "We need to trust God," they told one another. Then they saw "a horror on faces with wide mouths." Tower One had collapsed.

"My God!" Santiago cried.

"Lord, save my baby! Save my son!" his wife prayed.

They fled before the wave of debris back to the church.

Meanwhile, after an orderly exit from the school, the students were swept into the chaos of the streets. They stopped to stare at the burning buildings.

They jogged south to the southern tip of Manhattan. Matthew was a little ahead of Phillip. Then they heard a long rumble. Phillip yelled, "Is that thunder?" They all ducked.

After the thunder they started to hear metal cracking. "You could hear something bending, and then a sound like the cracking of millions of pieces of metal. A huge gray cloud started rolling toward us. It became darker and darker as it got closer," Phillip recalls.

The teachers said to turn back north to an emergency area. But the teachers were unfamiliar with the area, so Matthew took charge of his small group, shouting, "To the church!"

By this time Phillip and another girl were alone. He started running with her and praying. "I prayed God would keep me, and for my parents, that the police would tell them to go back home."

"A huge, boiling cloud of smoke and debris came like a fast-moving flood down a tunnel toward us," Matthew recalls. He led his group south, then around the tip of Manhattan toward the east side, the farthest that they could get from the towers.

Phillip, meanwhile, was bent down, covered with debris. He and his classmate staggered away. But "the smoke kept getting darker and darker until at times I couldn't even see my hand. . . . We couldn't run fast enough, and my classmate and I were starting to have trouble breathing."

Phillip prayed, "God, show me the way." He recalls that he became calm and knew God was drawing him to safety.

He saw a green sanitation van and ripped open the door, shoving his classmate and falling in behind her. "It was a miracle it was open. God was watching!" he thought. "We caught our breath for a few minutes as the debris stormed by."

Throwing open the door, the two students ran some more. "It was very hot in the smoke, and you just felt your throat clogging up, even with a cloth over your face."

Pastor Rivera was scrambling at the church. "Get food! Get tables!" he barked. He took chairs and water outside for the refugees. He scanned the crowds for any sign of his son and the other children.

"I remembered the black pastor who stood over a guy with outstretched arms during the Los Angeles riots. He was standing between the dead and the living. That was me. People needed someone to hang onto."

But Rivera was worried. Every 30 minutes or so, he would lock himself in his office to pace and cry out. "I did not see the walls or pictures," he says, during his prayers.

Across the street, the Santiagos felt helpless and despairing. Phillip's mother at one point prayed, "He is with you!"

"Then, my son walked in. Though he was snowy white, I knew who he was."

Phillip embraced his mother, saying, "I am okay! He was telling me where to go! God was telling me!"

A few minutes before, Matthew walked into the church with his teachers and students behind him, his hair filled with ash, pebbles, and concrete. He stood before his father amid a sea of people streaming by in silence.

The father reached over and hugged Matthew, and they wept. Matthew prayed his thanks.

That night, the Riveras formed a circle in their bedroom to thank God. Rivera closed, "Our goodbyes should be with the knowledge that life is fragile, and we won't always see each other again." Upstairs, the Santiagos looked at the dark clouds where the World Trade Center towers had stood. The father said, "We have to look for someone higher than the 110th floor."

The Riveras and Santiagos had their character tested. They say that they are ready for America's next tests.

A Time for Patriotism

Ask not what your country can do for you—ask what you can do for your country.

John F. Kennedy,
35th U.S. President

"A Patriotic Creed"

To serve my country day by day
At any humble post I may;
To honor and respect her flag,
To live the traits of which I brag;

To be American in deed
As well as in my printed creed
To stand for truth and honest toil,
To till my little patch of soil,

And keep in mind the debt I owe
To them who died that I may know
My country, prosperous and free,
And passed this heritage to me.

I always must in trouble's hour
Be guided by the men in power;
For God and country I must live,
My best for God and country give;

No act of mine that men may scan
Must shame the name American
To do my best and play my part
American in mind and heart;

To serve the flag and bravely stand
To guard the glory of my land;
To be American in deed:
God grant me strength to keep this creed!

Edgar A. Guest

*Great tragedy has come to us, and we
are meeting it with the best that is in
our country, with courage and concern
for others because this is America.
This is who we are.*

President George W. Bush
[radio address, September 15, 2001]

President George W. Bush's Address to Joint Session of Congress

Thursday, September 20, 2001

Mr. Speaker, Mr. President Pro Tempore, members of Congress, and fellow Americans:

In the normal course of events, presidents come to this chamber to report on the state of the Union. Tonight, no such report is needed. It has already been delivered by the American people.

We have seen it in the courage of passengers who rushed terrorists to save others on the ground. Passengers like an exceptional man named Todd Beamer. And would you please help me welcome his wife, Lisa Beamer, here tonight?

We have seen the state of our Union in the endurance of rescuers working past exhaustion.

We've seen the unfurling of flags, the lighting of candles, the giving of blood, the saying of prayers in English, Hebrew, and Arabic.

We have seen the decency of a loving and giving people who have made the grief of strangers their own.

My fellow citizens, for the last nine days, the entire world has seen for itself the state of our union, and it is strong.

Tonight, we are a country awakened to danger and called to defend freedom. Our grief has turned to anger and anger to resolution. Whether we bring our enemies to justice or bring justice to our enemies, justice will be done.

I thank the Congress for its leadership at such an important time.

All of America was touched on the evening of the tragedy to see Republicans and Democrats joined together on the steps of this Capitol singing "God Bless America."

And you did more than sing. You acted, by delivering $40 billion to rebuild our communities and meet the needs of our military. Speaker Hastert, Minority Leader Gephardt, Majority Leader Daschle, and Senator Lott, I thank you for your friendship, for your leadership, and for your service to our country.

And on behalf of the American people, I thank the world for its outpouring of support.

America will never forget the sounds of our national anthem playing at Buckingham Palace, on the streets of Paris, and at Berlin's Brandenburg Gate.

We will not forget South Korean children gathering to pray outside our embassy in Seoul, or the prayers of sympathy offered at a mosque in Cairo.

We will not forget moments of silence and days of mourning in Australia and Africa and Latin America.

Nor will we forget the citizens of eighty other nations who died with our own. Dozens of Pakistanis, more than 130 Israelis, more than 250 citizens of India, men and women from El Salvador, Iran, Mexico, and Japan, and hundreds of British citizens.

America has no truer friend than Great Britain.

Once again, we are joined together in a great cause.

I'm so honored the British prime minister has crossed an ocean to show his unity with America.

Thank you for coming, friend.

On September 11, enemies of freedom committed an act of war against our country. Americans have known wars, but for the past 136 years they have been wars on foreign soil, except for one Sunday in 1941. Americans have known the casualties of war, but not at the center of a great city on a peaceful morning.

Americans have known surprise attacks, but never before on thousands of civilians.

All of this was brought upon us in a single day, and night fell on a different world, a world where freedom itself is under attack.

Americans have many questions tonight. Americans are asking, "Who attacked our country?"

The evidence we have gathered all points to a collection of loosely affiliated terrorist organizations known as Al Qaeda. They are some of the murderers indicted for bombing American embassies in Tanzania and Kenya and responsible for bombing the USS Cole.

Al Qaeda is to terror what the Mafia is to crime. But its goal is not making money; its goal is remaking the world and imposing its radical beliefs on people everywhere.

The terrorists practice a fringe form of Islamic extremism that has been rejected by Muslim scholars and the vast majority of Muslim clerics—a fringe movement that perverts the peaceful teachings of Islam.

The terrorists' directive commands them to kill Christians and Jews, to kill all Americans and make no distinctions among military and civilians, including women and children.

This group and its leader, a person named Osama bin Laden, are linked to many other organizations in different countries, including the Egyptian Islamic Jihad, the Islamic Movement of Uzbekistan.

There are thousands of these terrorists in more than sixty countries.

They are recruited from their own nations and neighborhoods and brought to camps in places like Afghanistan where they are trained in the tactics of terror. They are sent back to their homes or sent to hide in countries around the world to plot evil and destruction.

The leadership of Al Qaeda has great influence in Afghanistan and supports the Taliban regime in controlling most of that country. In Afghanistan, we see Al Qaeda's vision for the world. Afghanistan's people have been brutalized; many are starving and many have fled.

Women are not allowed to attend school. You can be jailed for owning a television. Religion can be practiced only as their leaders dictate. A man can be jailed in Afghanistan if his beard is not long enough.

The United States respects the people of Afghanistan— after all, we are currently its largest source of humanitarian aid—but we condemn the Taliban regime.

It is not only repressing its own people, it is threatening people everywhere by sponsoring and sheltering and supplying terrorists.

By aiding and abetting murder, the Taliban regime is committing murder. And tonight the United States of America makes the following demands on the Taliban:

Deliver to United States authorities all of the leaders of Al Qaeda who hide in your land.

Release all foreign nationals, including American citizens you have unjustly imprisoned. Protect foreign journalists, diplomats, and aid workers in your country.

Close immediately and permanently every terrorist training camp in Afghanistan. And hand over every terrorist and every person and their support structure to appropriate authorities.

Give the United States full access to terrorist training camps, so we can make sure they are no longer operating.

These demands are not open to negotiation or discussion.

The Taliban must act and act immediately.

They will hand over the terrorists, or they will share in their fate.

I also want to speak tonight directly to Muslims throughout the world. We respect your faith. It's practiced freely by many millions of Americans and by millions more in countries that America counts as friends. Its teachings are good and peaceful, and those who commit evil in the name of Allah blaspheme the name of Allah.

The terrorists are traitors to their own faith, trying, in effect, to hijack Islam itself.

The enemy of America is not our many Muslim friends. It is not our many Arab friends. Our enemy is a radical network of terrorists and every government that supports them.

Our war on terror begins with Al Qaeda, but it does not end there.

It will not end until every terrorist group of global reach has been found, stopped, and defeated.

Americans are asking, "Why do they hate us?"

They hate what they see right here in this chamber: a democratically-elected government. Their leaders are self-appointed. They hate our freedoms: our freedom of religion, our freedom of speech, our freedom to vote and assemble and disagree with each other.

They want to overthrow existing governments in many Muslim countries such as Egypt, Saudi Arabia, and Jordan. They want to drive Israel out of the Middle East. They want to drive Christians and Jews out of vast regions of Asia and Africa.

These terrorists kill not merely to end lives, but to disrupt and end a way of life. With every atrocity, they hope that America grows fearful, retreating from the world and forsaking our friends. They stand against us because we stand in their way.

We're not deceived by their pretenses to piety.

We have seen their kind before. They're the heirs of all the murderous ideologies of the twentieth century. By sacrificing human life to serve their radical visions, by abandoning every value except the will to power, they follow in the path of fascism, Nazism, and totalitarianism. And they will follow that path all the way to where it ends in history's unmarked grave of discarded lies.

Americans are asking, "How will we fight and win this war?"

We will direct every resource at our command—every means of diplomacy, every tool of intelligence, every instrument of law enforcement, every financial influence, and every necessary weapon of war—to the destruction and to the defeat of the global terror network.

Now, this war will not be like the war against Iraq a decade ago, with a decisive liberation of territory and a swift conclusion. It will not look like the air war above Kosovo two years ago, where no ground troops were used and not a single American was lost in combat.

Our response involves far more than instant retaliation and isolated strikes. Americans should not expect one battle, but a lengthy campaign unlike any other we have ever seen. It may include dramatic strikes visible on TV and covert operations secret even in success.

We will starve terrorists of funding, turn them one against another, drive them from place to place until there is no refuge or no rest.

And we will pursue nations that provide aid or safe haven to terrorism. Every nation in every region now has a decision to make: Either you are with us or you are with the terrorists.

From this day forward, any nation that continues to harbor or support terrorism will be regarded by the United States as a hostile regime. Our nation has been put on notice; we're not immune from attack. We will take defensive measures against terrorism to protect Americans.

Today, dozens of federal departments and agencies, as well as state and local governments, have responsibilities affecting homeland security.

These efforts must be coordinated at the highest level. So tonight, I announce the creation of a Cabinet-level position reporting directly to me, the Office of Homeland Security.

And tonight, I also announce a distinguished American to lead this effort, to strengthen American security: a military veteran, an effective governor, a true patriot, a trusted friend, Pennsylvania's Tom Ridge.

He will lead, oversee, and coordinate a comprehensive national strategy to safeguard our country against terrorism and respond to any attacks that may come.

These measures are essential. The only way to defeat terrorism as a threat to our way of life is to stop it, eliminate it, and destroy it where it grows.

Many will be involved in this effort, from FBI agents, to intelligence operatives, to the reservists we have called to active duty. All deserve our thanks, and all have our prayers.

And tonight a few miles from the damaged Pentagon, I have a message for our military: Be ready. I have called the armed forces to alert, and there is a reason.

The hour is coming when America will act, and you will make us proud.

This is not, however, just America's fight. And what is at stake is not just America's freedom.

This is the world's fight. This is civilization's fight. This is the fight of all who believe in progress and pluralism, tolerance and freedom.

We ask every nation to join us.

We will ask and we will need the help of police forces, intelligence service, and banking systems around the world. The United States is grateful that many nations and many international organizations have already responded with sympathy and with support—nations from Latin America to Asia to Africa to Europe to the Islamic world.

Perhaps the NATO charter reflects best the attitude of the world: An attack on one is an attack on all. The civilized world is rallying to America's side.

They understand that if this terror goes unpunished, their own cities, their own citizens may be next. Terror unanswered cannot only bring down buildings, it can threaten the stability of legitimate governments.

And you know what? We're not going to allow it.

Americans are asking, "What is expected of us?"

I ask you to live your lives and hug your children.

I know many citizens have fears tonight, and I ask you to be calm and resolute, even in the face of a continuing threat.

I ask you to uphold the values of America and remember why so many have come here.

We're in a fight for our principles, and our first responsibility is to live by them. No one should be singled out for unfair treatment or unkind words because of their ethnic background or religious faith.

I ask you to continue to support the victims of this tragedy with your contributions. Those who want to give can go to a central source of information, Libertyunites.org, to find the names of groups providing direct help in New York, Pennsylvania, and Virginia.

The thousands of FBI agents who are now at work in this investigation may need your cooperation, and I ask you to give it. I ask for your patience with the delays and inconveniences that may accompany tighter security and for your patience in what will be a long struggle.

I ask your continued participation and confidence in the American economy. Terrorists attacked a symbol of American prosperity; they did not touch its source.

America is successful because of the hard work and creativity and enterprise of our people. These were the true strengths of our economy before September 11, and they are our strengths today.

And finally, please continue praying for the victims of terror and their families, for those in uniform and for our great country. Prayer has comforted us in sorrow and will help strengthen us for the journey ahead.

Tonight I thank my fellow Americans for what you have already done and for what you will do.

And ladies and gentlemen of the Congress, I thank you, their representatives, for what you have already done and for what we will do together.

Tonight we face new and sudden national challenges.

We will come together to improve air safety, to dramatically expand the number of air marshals on domestic flights, and to take new measures to prevent hijacking.

We will come together to promote stability and keep our airlines flying with direct assistance during this emergency.

We will come together to give law enforcement the additional tools it needs to track down terror here at home.

We will come together to strengthen our intelligence capabilities to know the plans of terrorists before they act and to find them before they strike.

We will come together to take active steps that strengthen America's economy and put our people back to work.

Tonight, we welcome two leaders who embody the extraordinary spirit of all New Yorkers, Governor George Pataki and Mayor Rudolph Giuliani.

As a symbol of America's resolve, my administration will work with Congress and these two leaders to show the world that we will rebuild New York City.

After all that has just passed, all the lives taken and all the possibilities and hopes that died with them, it is natural to wonder if America's future is one of fear.

Some speak of an age of terror. I know there are struggles ahead and dangers to face. But this country will define our times, not be defined by them.

As long as the United States of America is determined and strong, this will not be an age of terror. This will be an age of liberty here and across the world.

Great harm has been done to us. We have suffered great loss. And in our grief and anger we have found our mission and our moment.

Freedom and fear are at war. The advance of human freedom, the great achievement of our time, and the great hope of every time, now depends on us.

Our nation, this generation, will lift the dark threat of violence from our people and our future. We will rally the world to this cause by our efforts, by our courage. We will not tire, we will not falter, and we will not fail.

It is my hope that in the months and years ahead life will return almost to normal. We'll go back to our lives and routines, and that is good.

Even grief recedes with time and grace.

But our resolve must not pass. Each of us will remember what happened that day and to whom it happened. We will remember the moment the news came, where we were and what we were doing.

Some will remember an image of a fire or story or rescue. Some will carry memories of a face and a voice gone forever.

And I will carry this. It is the police shield of a man named George Howard who died at the World Trade Center trying to save others.

It was given to me by his mom, Arlene, as a proud memorial to her son. It is my reminder of lives that ended and a task that does not end.

I will not forget the wound to our country and those who inflicted it. I will not yield, I will not rest, I will not relent in waging this struggle for freedom and security for the American people.

The course of this conflict is not known, yet its outcome is certain. Freedom and fear, justice and cruelty, have always been at war, and we know that God is not neutral between them.

Fellow citizens, we'll meet violence with patient justice, assured of the rightness of our cause and confident of the victories to come.

In all that lies before us, may God grant us wisdom, and may He watch over the United States of America. Thank you.

"See It Through"

There are many to cheer when the battle begins,
There are many to shout for the right;
There are many to rail at the world and its sins,
But few have the grit for the fight.
There are thousands to start with a rush for the fray
When the fighting seems easy to do,
But when danger is present and rough is the way,
The few have to see the job through.

It is easy to quit with a battle unwon,
It is hard to press on to success;
It is easy to stop with a purpose undone,
It is hard to encounter distress.
And many will march when the roadway is clear
And the glorious goal is in view,
But the many, too often, when dangers appear,
Aren't willing to see the fight through.

They weaken in spirit when trials grow great,
They flinch at the clashing of steel;
They talk of the strength of the foe at the gate
And whine at the hurts that they feel.
They begin to regret having ventured for right,
They sigh that they dared to be true,

They haven't the heart they once had for the fight.
They don't want to see the job through.

We have set out to battle for justice and truth,
We have fearful disasters to meet;
We shall weep for the best of our manliest youth,
We shall suffer the pangs of defeat.
But let us stand firm for the cause that we plead,
Let the many be brave with the few;
The cry of the quitter let none of us heed
Till we've done what we started to do.

by Edgar A. Guest

Our Darkest Day; Our Finest Hour

By Mayor Rudy Giuliani

On September 11, New York City suffered the darkest day in our long history. The destruction of the World Trade Center, and the resulting loss of thousands of lives, has broken our City's heart. But our heart still beats and our City remains strong. We will emerge from this stronger than we have ever been before.

This vicious, unprovoked attack on our City, and our Nation, demonstrates the depths of human cowardice and cruelty. Yet the reaction of New Yorkers to this tragedy has shown us the heights of human generosity and courage. Within moments after the first plane struck, ordinary men and women showed extraordinary bravery in assisting one another to safety, even at the cost of their own lives. Our Fire Fighters and Police Officers have personified courage, and though the losses to their ranks have been terrible, they have set the example for the rest of us by continuing to work with renewed vigor.

The Fire Department, in particular, has suffered greatly. More than 300 members of the Department are dead or missing as of this writing, and we have already held funerals for three of the most beloved and valued members of New York's Bravest: Chief Peter Ganci; First Deputy Commissioner William Feehan; and Father Mychal Judge. These legendary leaders and their many courageous fallen colleagues will never be forgotten.

This tragedy, along with the nearly simultaneous bombing of the Pentagon in Washington and the crash of a hijacked commercial plane near Pittsburgh, has touched the lives of millions of people throughout our City, across the Nation, and around the world. Family members, friends, and co-workers have been suddenly taken from us. This enormous loss provokes our sadness, and it also stirs a sense of outrage and anger. President Bush is right to call this an act of war. He is also right to declare that the terrorist enemies of the United States will face retaliation. Basic justice—and the national interest—demand no less.

Yet even as we mourn our dead and prepare for what could be a long and bitter war against an elusive enemy, let us always remember that our greatest national strengths are our openness, our diversity, our inclusiveness, and our freedom. These are the assets that our terrorist foes seek to destroy, but these are also the values that will guarantee our eventual and total victory. The people of the City of New York will demonstrate that we are stronger than these barbarians. We are not going to participate in group blame or group hatred, because those are the sicknesses that caused this tragedy. Our City is going to continue to honor its immigrant heritage. Through the strength of our example, we are going to send the message that life in our City goes on, undeterred. We will continue to embody the highest ideals of America.

I have always had full confidence in the people of this City, and that confidence has risen even higher as I have watched the behavior of New Yorkers in the wake of this tragedy. They evacuated the scene of destruction in good order; they almost immediately formed long lines to donate blood; they have made generous corporate and individual donations of money and supplies; they have offered welcome encouragement and solace to the relatives of the missing and to our exhausted rescue workers. We are a united City, and I have never been so proud to be a New Yorker.

Home of the Brave

By Mariby B. Johns

While listening to British citizens sing "The Star-Spangled Banner" during a memorial service in London, I had, for the first time, an emotional appreciation for the words, "O'er the land of the free and the home of the brave."

I thought of the bravery of the firefighters who ran up the stairs, toward danger, past people streaming down the steps trying to escape the fires and devastation. I thought of the police officers, the rescue workers, the doctors, and ordinary citizens who put themselves at risk to help others escape or to help find victims buried in the rubble.

In the past, the words of our anthem had seemed abstract, referring only to bravery in battles long over. But last week's bravery, stemming from care and concern for others, was happening over and over before our eyes.

New York, Pennsylvania, and Washington certainly have been homes of the brave during this horrific time. I felt proud of the importance that our country places on freedom. Although that freedom is part of what makes us vulnerable to perverse fanatics, it is what keeps us a strong nation.

"The Star Spangled Banner"

by Francis Scott Key

Oh, say can you see, by the dawn's early light, What so proudly we hailed at the twilight's last gleaming? Whose broad stripes and bright stars, thro' the perilous fight, O'er the ramparts we watched, were so gallantly streaming?

And the rockets' red glare, the bombs bursting in air, Gave proof thro' the night that our flag was still there. Oh, say does that Star-spangled Banner yet wave O'er the land of the free, and the home of the brave?

On the shore, dimly seen thro' the mists of the deep, Where the foe's haughty host in dread silence reposes, What is that which the breeze, o'er the towering steep, As it fitfully blows, half conceals, half discloses?

Now it catches the gleam of the morning's first beam, In full glory reflected, now shines on the stream: 'Tis the Star spangled-Banner; oh long may it wave O'er the land of the free, and the home of the brave.

And where is that band, who so vauntingly swore That the havoc of war and the battle's confusion, A home and a country should leave us no more? Their blood has washed out their foul footsteps' pollution;

No refuge could save the hireling and slave From the terror of flight or the gloom of the grave; And the Star spangled-Banner in triumph doth wave O'er the land of the free, and the home of the brave.

Oh, thus be it ever when free men shall stand Between their loved homes and war's desolation; Blest with victory and peace, may the Heav'n rescued land Praise the Power that hath made and preserved us a nation.

Then conquer we must, when our cause it is just; And this be our motto: "In God is our trust!" And the Star-spangled Banner in triumph shall wave O'er the land of the free, and the home of the brave.

"Show the Flag"

Show the flag and let it wave
As a symbol of the brave;
Let it float upon the breeze
As a sign for each who sees
That beneath it, where it rides,
Loyalty today abides.

Show the flag and signify
That it wasn't born to die;
Let its colors speak for you
That you still are standing true,
True in sight of God and man
To the work that flag began.

Show the flag that all may see
That you serve humanity.
Let it whisper to the breeze
That comes singing through the trees
That whatever storms descend
You'll be faithful to the end.

Show the flag and let it fly,
Cheering every passerby —-
Men that may have stepped aside,

May have lost their old-time pride,
May behold it there, and then
Consecrate themselves again.

Show the flag! The day is gone
When men blindly hurry on
Serving only gods of gold;
Now the spirit that was cold
Warms again to courage fine.
Show the flag and fall in line!

New Yorkers Discover Their Inner American

By Jeremy Simon

NEW YORK—Earlier this week, I looked out my apartment window on the Upper West Side of Manhattan, eight miles uptown from the World Trade Center, and saw something that may forever alter my view of New York. Two American flags hung from the window of the building across the street, and it took me a few seconds to realize that what I was seeing was quite unusual.

When I went downtown later, it became impossible not to notice the flags. Old Glory hung from the rafters of supermarkets, stood stiff on the antennae of taxicabs, and draped across the shoulders of couples. Everywhere I looked, I saw red, white, and blue backpack patches and T-shirts. And then there were a few American flag bandannas, into which New Yorkers breathed to protect their lungs against the chemical, unworldly air just two miles north of where two 757s had knocked out the city's two front teeth.

To rally 'round the flag is the American thing to do in times of strife. But on any given day in New York, I probably see more Puerto Rican or Colombian or Cuban flags than American flags. I wouldn't even know where in New York I could buy an American flag. On reconsideration, I might try Times Square, where the tourists go.

It's not that the born Americans among us explicitly deny their national heritage. More likely, New Yorkers consider American patriotism a sentimental weakness, a fashion faux-pas, or even an incidental allegiance. During peacetime, New York is less like a major American city and more like a rogue nation, a self-sufficient entity with a collective ego (and a gross metropolitan product) that far exceeds that of several genuine rogue nations. We have mastered the fine art of tuning out the uncontrollable and the unnecessary. When we fold our pizza slices in the middle, we're not the ones eating it differently— *you* are.

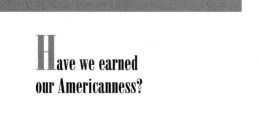

Have we earned our Americanness?

But this is no longer peacetime. For the first time in generations, New York's illusion that it is alone in the world has been undeniably obliterated. We are now clinging desperately to the expectation that America's government and values are superior to those of its enemy, whomever it may be. Demonstrably, we are discovering and asserting our Americanness.

Have we earned our Americanness?

In ways, the tragedy underlines what we have always suspected—that life in New York is of a greater magnitude, both in its successes and its disasters. But most New

Yorkers, including myself, first experienced this tragedy just as you did: on television and on the Internet. When the planes hit, it was a beautiful day in uptown Manhattan. We could not see the smoke, which initially blew southward off the island, and it was even possible to pretend it happened somewhere else.

That changed later, when our phone calls failed to go through for three hours, and the wind shifted and blew the concrete ash uptown, and we were evacuated from the city's major train station because a dog got excited about an unattended box two blocks away. What started as a media event became a nuisance, then a horror, and finally a condition.

We realized—we who have perfected the thousand-yard subway stare and the ya-better-not-be-wantin-change walk—that we would have to listen to strangers, be patient, open our eyes to need.

The initial steps have been difficult, but we can blame it on circumstance. There have been the clumsy greetings with acquaintances on the street. The initial reserve. The inevitable, "Did you know anybody? Is everyone OK?" The tongue on the roof of the mouth. The diplomatic "Well . . . mostly."

The one-upmanship urge—the urge that before would might make us think "What's *he* got to mourn about? *I* lost three friends here, and all he lost was some guy he hasn't talked to since law school!"—has dissipated. There is a refreshing understanding that we have all lost something here.

And who knew we had all these brave cops and firefighters?

I think we have struggled most with our helplessness. After all, they're right down there! We can see the smoke! God knows, we can taste it! Of course, we wouldn't be allowed to drag bodies from the rubble, but isn't there something we can do? After all, we're New Yorkers! We tried to give blood, we tried, we tried. But we all tried at once, and any time New Yorkers try to do one thing all at once, it's too much. On the news, they said they were looking for donations. Gas masks . . . Ace bandages . . . dog boots!? Who has extra dog boots?

So instead, we listen silently, stand in the streets or on the piers, and stare downtown into nothing, hug each other, and wave our flags.

"The patriotism, it's just stunning, isn't it? It's a wonderful thing," a colleague of mine recently said to me. The patriotism is certainly abundant, but its knee-jerkiness scares me. When we run out of other things to say about the disaster, we talk about retaliation. "We've got to show them what we're made of!"

But when we say "we," do we really mean "they," the people down in that place called Washington (where they also had a disaster, we have heard)? Or some kids with crew cuts in Oklahoma or North Carolina, who will likely be the ones sent to fight our fight?

We have been broken here, and when we rebuild, we had better not build the walls too thick. Whether we acknowledge it or not, New York is a part of America. Those with grudges against this country already recognize this.

But we will soon again have our markets, our fashion industries, our media empires to tend to. Very soon, New Yorkers will again receive news from another part of this country, and for once we will be relieved that the spotlight is somewhere else. I hope that we're not too cool for our American flags, on that unimaginable but not-far-off day, when they are hoisted again from half mast to full.

Stars and Stripes

How glorious has been the history of our flag! There is not such another banner in all the world that has carried such hope, such grandeur of spirit, such soul-inspiring truth, as our dear old American Flag! Made by liberty, made for liberty, nourished in its spirit, and carried in its service.

Rev. Henry Ward Beecher

The flag is the one focus in which all unite in reverential devotion.

Major General Arthur MacArthur

What the cross is to faith, the flag is to freedom.

Anonymous

Let the flag of our country wave from the spire of every church in the land, with nothing above it but the cross of Christ.

Rev. E. A. Anderson

"Our Duty to Our Flag"

Less hate and greed
Is what we need
And more of service true;
More men to love
The flag above
And keep it first in view.

Less boast and brag
About the flag,
More faith in what it means;
More heads erect,
More self-respect,
Less talk of war machines.

The time to fight
To keep it bright
Is not along the way,
Nor 'cross the foam,
But here at home
Within ourselves—today.

'Tis we must love

That flag above
With all our might and main;
For from our hands—
Not distant lands—
Shall come dishonor's stain.

If that flag be
Dishonored, we
Have done it—not the foe;
If it shall fall,
We, first of all,
Shall have to strike the blow.

Edgar A. Guest

The American Flag

By Emily Katharine Ide

June 14, 1777, is the date that marks the beginning of the authentic history of our flag and when the American Congress adopted the following resolution:

"Resolved—that the flag of the thirteen United States be thirteen stripes, alternate red and white, that the union be thirteen stars, white in a blue field, representing a new constellation."

The American Flag represents a glorious Land of Liberty and Union, the dear purchase of generations past. It represents a government "of the people, by the people and for the people" who enjoy justice, freedom, and equality of rights. Our flag means Americanism. It stands for civilization, for our past heroism, our present power and prosperity, and for future achievements and progress. The Stars and Stripes represents a great republic which was ordained by God. We are reaping the harvest sowed by self-denial, hardship, and the manifold sufferings of our forefathers. We are enjoying a prosperity unparalleled in the history of the world. Our labor and industry have been a source of luxury and extravagance that begets recklessness, idleness, and vice. Let us not forget that in order to insure continued independence and prosperity, we must maintain honor; this means the conscientious exercising of all duties, by those officials elected by the people to guard our rights and interests. We must insist on honor in our legislative chamber; inflexibility in our courts of law; truth in our public press; the regulation of the interests existing between capital and labor; and a sense of stewardship on the part of the rich. The flag of our great republic calls for these high ideals, and towards the maintenance of these principles every patriotic American has much to do. Let us bear in mind the quotation "that eternal vigilance is the price of liberty," and that only by intelligence, sacrifice, progressions, and preparedness, can we perpetuate the power of the Stars and Stripes.

From the bosom of the future, posterity calls out to us, and generations to come hold us responsible for the sacred trust of this great republic and the honor of the flag that now protects 100 million people. When the Stars and Stripes floats about our heads, we feel its living presence in our hearts and that inspiration which has always led us on to victory and glory. Beneath the illumination of its stars, let us walk our course of life, giving thanks not only to God Almighty for this privilege, but to those martyrs who died that we might enjoy liberty. Flag of our great republic may you forever wave over "the holy temple of American Liberty!"

Emily Katherine Ide, *The History and Significance of the American Flag*, Huntington Art Press, 1917.

Billows of smoke pour from the World Trade Center Buildings in New York Tuesday, Sept.11, 2001. Planes crashed into the upper floors of both World Trade Center towers minutes apart in a horrific scene of explosions and fires that left gaping holes in the 110-story buildings. The Empire State building is seen in the foreground.

AP/Wide World Photos

Smoke rises from the Pentagon in Arlington, Va. Tuesday, Sept. 11, 2001 as members of the Fairfax County Search and Rescue team approach after a terrorist attack.

AP/Wide World Photos

Engine 28 firefighter Mike Kehoe, from Staten Island, assists in the evacuation effort in a stairwell of Tower One Tuesday, Sept. 11, 2001 during the attacks on the World Trade Center towers in New York. These pictures were shot by a man who had an office on the 71st floor of the building. Both Kehoe and the photographer escaped before the towers collapsed.

AP/Wide World Photos

Thick smoke billows into the sky from the area behind the Statue of Liberty where the World Trade Center towers stood Tuesday, Sept. 11, 2001. The towers collapsed after terrorists crashed two planes into them.

AP/Wide World Photos

President Bush sits with his National Security Council during a meeting in the Cabinet Room of the White House, Wednesday, Sept. 12, 2001. From left to right, CIA Director George Tentent, Secretary of Defense Donald Rumsfeld, Secretary of State Colin Powell, President Bush, Vice President Dick Cheney and Chairman of the Joint Chiefs of Staff Gen. Henry Shelton, and National Security Advisor Condoleeza Rice.

AP/Wide World Photos

Firefighters unfurl an American flag from the roof of the Pentagon Wednesday, Sept. 12, 2001, as President Bush visits the area of the Pentagon damaged by terrorists.
AP/Wide World Photo

A message written in the children's area of the Oklahoma City National Memorial: From a family member to a family member, my heart hurts deeply. We love you NYC and DC. My Prayers are with you all.
AP/Wide World Photos

As rescue efforts continue in the rubble of the World Trade Center, President Bush puts his arm around firefighter Bob Beckwith while standing in front of the World Trade Center debris during a tour of the devastation, Friday, September 14, 2001. Bush is standing on a burned fire truck.
AP/Wide World Photos

Rev. Mychal Judge's helmet is placed on his coffin as representatives of various fire brigades in New Jersey form an honor guard at the Franciscan Fathers burial site in Totawa, N.J., Saturday, Sept. 15, 2001. Judge, 68, died Tuesday as he was administering last rites to a firefighter mortally injured in the attack on the World Trade Center. (Story on page 43.)

A firefighter is seen in the wreckage of the World Trade Center in New York, Friday., Sept. 14, 2001.

AP/Wide World Photos

Diane Gorumba, of Brooklyn, N.Y., who lost her grandfather, father, and brother in the past year, is walked down the aisle by New York City Mayor Rudolph Giuliani, Sunday, Sept. 16, 2001 at St. James Lutheran Church in Brooklyn. At her brother, firefighter Michael Gorumba's funeral last month, Gorumba's mother asked the Mayor to accompany her daughter down the aisle. Michael Gorumba was a firefighter who died of a heart attack while fighting a fire in Staten Island. (Story on page 111.)

AP/Wide World Photos

As U.S. troops and warplanes move into position, President Bush addresses a Joint Session of Congress on Capitol Hill to prepare Americans for a long, deadly and often covert war against the elusive terrorists. Sitting behind Bush are Sen. Robert Byrd, president pro-tem of the Senate, and House Speaker Dennis Hastert. (Address on page 133.) AP/Wide World Photos

Lisa Beamer, widow of Todd Beamer, who died on United Airline Flight 93 that crashed in Pennsylvania is applauded on Capitol Hill after being recognized by President Bush during his address before a joint session of Congress. (Story on page 35.) AP/Wide World Photos

The Rev. Brian Jordan (second from left) blesses a cross of steel beams found amid the rubble of the World Trade Center by a laborer two days after the collapse of the twin towers. Other rescue and construction workers join Jordan for the ceremony. A protective mesh hangs on the building in the background. AP/Wide World Photos

(above) A mother and her daughter pause at a memorial on the access road to the crash site of United Flight 93 in Shanksville, Pa., Sunday, Sept. 23, 2001.
AP/Wide World Photos

(center, left) A New York Police officer prays in St. Paul's Chapel in New York near the World Trade Center crash site. The church dates back to the 1700s.   AP/Wide World Photos

(center, right) Navy Seaman 1st Class Cean Whitmarsh, looks over memorial notes left at a makeshift memorial near the Pentagon in Washington DC. A Pentagon ceiling fell on him and his co-workers after the attack on Sept, 11 and he is credited with helping save as many as a dozen of his colleagues.   AP/Wide World Photos

(bottom) A man stops to pray among the 5,000 crosses his church, the Bible Baptist Church, had placed in a field in Guthrie, Okla. The church placed the crosses to show the number of people missing in New York City. There were 5,000 missing when the idea was created. The church said they would paint the name of victims on the crosses as they learn names.
AP/Wide World Photos

(top, left) American flags and a sign reading "We Will Never Forget" hang from the heavily damaged American Express building on West Street across from the site of the terrorist attack on the World Trade Center in lower Manhattan Monday, Sept. 24, 2001. Part of the structure of one of the destroyed World Trade Center twin towers can be seen in the foreground.   AP/Wide World Photos

(top, right) Disaster relief workers share in a moment of silence during a prayer service Sunday, Oct. 7, 2001 at ground zero, in New York, where the World Trade Center once stood. Nearly four weeks after terrorist attacks leveled the area, a prayer service was held under chilly but sunny skies for workers at the site.   AP/Wide World Photos

A soldier kisses his bride after the couple was married, during a double wedding, Wednesday, Oct. 10, 2001 at the Army Reserve Training Center in Zanesville, Ohio. Both couples arranged their weddings after the grooms were called for duty.
AP/Wide World Photos

A boy is held up by his father while waving the American flag Sunday, September 23, 2001 during a prayer service at Yankee Stadium in New York.
AP/Wide World Photos

A father holds his daughter during the national anthem Sunday Sept. 16, 2001, at Bayside Park in Miami. Hundreds of South Florida citizens gathered at a candlelight vigil to show their support for the victims in New York, Washington DC, and Pennsylvania.
AP/Wide World Photos

The Flag

Capt. John S. McCain

L et me tell you what I think about our Pledge of Allegiance, our flag, and our country.

As you may know, I spent five and one half years as a prisoner of war during the Vietnam War. In the early years of our imprisonment, the NVA kept us in solitary confinement or two or three to a cell. In 1971 the NVA moved us from these conditions of isolation into large rooms with as many as thirty to forty men to a room. This was, as you can imagine, a wonderful change and was a direct result of the efforts of millions of Americans on behalf of a few hundred POWs 10,000 miles from home.

One of the men who moved into my room was a young man named Mike Christian.

Mike came from a small town near Selma, Alabama. He didn't wear a pair of shoes until he was thirteen years old. At seventeen, he enlisted in the US Navy. He later earned a commission by going to Officer Training School. Then he became a Naval Flight Officer and was shot down and captured in 1967. Mike had a keen and deep appreciation of the opportunities this country, and our military, provide for people who want to work and want to succeed. As part of the change in treatment, the Vietnamese allowed some prisoners to receive packages from home. In some of these packages were handkerchiefs, scarves, and other items of clothing. Mike got himself a bamboo needle.

Over a period of a couple of months, he created an American flag and sewed it on the inside of his shirt. Every afternoon, before we had a bowl of soup, we would hang Mike's shirt on the wall of the cell and say the Pledge of Allegiance. I know the Pledge of Allegiance may not seem the most important part of our day now, but I can assure you that in that stark cell, it was indeed the most important and meaningful event .

One day the Vietnamese searched our cell, as they did periodically, and discovered Mike's shirt with the flag sewn inside, and removed it. That evening they returned, opened the door of the cell, and for the benefit of all us, beat Mike Christian severely for the next couple of hours.

Then, they opened the door of the cell and threw him in. We cleaned him up as well as we could. The cell in which we lived had a concrete slab in the middle on which we slept. Four naked light bulbs hung in each corner of the room. As said, we tried to clean up Mike as well as we could. After the excitement died down, I looked in the corner of the room, and sitting there beneath that dim light bulb with a piece of red cloth, another shirt and his bamboo needle, was my friend, Mike Christian. He was sitting there with his eyes almost shut from the beating he had received, making another American flag.

He was not making the flag because it made Mike Christian feel better. He was making that flag because he knew how important it was to us to be able to pledge our allegiance to our flag and country.

You must remember our duty, our honor, and our country. We must never forget the sacrifice and courage that thousands of Americans have made to build our nation and promote freedom around the world.

From a speech made by Capt. John S. McCain, US, (Rep) who represents Arizona in the U.S. Senate:

Pledge of Allegiance

I pledge allegiance to the flag of the United States of America, and to the republic for which it stands, one nation under God, indivisible with liberty and justice for all.

"The Call"

Some will heed the call to arms,
But all must heed the call to grit;
The dreamers on the distant farms
Must rally now to do their bit.
The whirring lathes in factories great
Will sing the martial songs of strife;
Upon the emery wheel of fate
We're grinding now the nation's life.

The call is not alone to guns,
This is not but a battle test;
The world has summoned free men's sons
In every field to do their best.
The call has come to every man
To reach the summit of his powers;
To stand to service where he can,
A mighty duty now is ours.

We must be stalwarts in the field
Where peace has always kept her throne,
No door against the need is sealed,
No man today can live alone.
The young apprentice at the bench,
The wise inventor, old and gray,

Serve with the soldier in the trench,
All warriors for the better day.

Oh, man of science, unto you
The call for service now has come!
Mechanic, banker, lawyer, too,
Have you not heard the stirring drum?
Oh, humble digger in the ditch,
Bend to your spade and do your best,
And prove America is rich
In manhood fine for every test.

Each man beneath the starry flag
Must live his noblest through the strife,
If tyranny is not to dray
Into the mire the best of life.
Though some will wear our uniform,
We face today a common fate
And all must bravely breast the storm
And heed the call for courage great.

Edgar A. Guest

Presidential Wisdom

George Washington (1st U.S. President): "We ought not to look back unless it is to derive useful lessons from past errors."

John Adams (2nd U.S. President): "There is nothing so likely to produce peace as to be well prepared to meet an enemy."

Thomas Jefferson (3rd U.S. President): "No man has a natural right to commit aggression on the equal rights of another."

James Monroe (5th U.S. President): "Our great resources . . . are more especially to be found in the virtue, patriotism, and intelligence of our fellow-citizens."

Andrew Jackson (7th U.S. President): "I cannot be intimidated from doing that which my judgment and conscience tell me is right by any earthly power."

William Harrison (9th U.S. President): "The strongest of all governments is that which is most free."

John Tyler (10th U.S. President): "The great primary and controlling interest of the American people is union . . . union founded in an attachment of . . . individuals for each other."

Millard Fillmore (13th U.S. President): "The man who can look upon a crisis without being willing to offer himself upon the altar of his country is not fit for public trust."

James Buchanan (15th U.S. President): "Liberty must be allowed to work out its natural results; and these will . . . astonish the world."

Abraham Lincoln (16th U.S. President): "Let us have faith that right make might. . . . Having thus chosen our course . . . let us renew our trust in God and go forward without fear."

Rutherford B. Hayes (19th U.S. President): "It is now true that this is God's Country, if equal rights—a fair start and an equal chance in the race of life are everywhere secured to all."

James Garfield (20th U.S. President): "Justice and goodwill will outlast passion."

Chester Arthur (21st U.S. President): "Men may die, but the fabrics of our free institutions remain unshaken."

William McKinley (25th U.S. President): "In time of darkest defeat, victory may be nearest."

Theodore Roosevelt (26th U.S. President): "The first requisite of a good citizen . . . is that he shall be able and willing to pull his weight."

Woodrow Wilson (28th U.S. President): "One cool judgment is worth a thousand hasty counsels; the thing to do is to supply light and not heat."

Warren Harding (29th U.S. President): "America's present need is not heroics but healing."

Calvin Coolidge (30th U.S. President): "No person was ever honored for what he received. Honor has been the reward for what he gave."

Franklin D. Roosevelt (32nd U.S. President): "The only thing we have to fear is fear itself."

Dwight Eisenhower (34th U.S. President): "Accomplishment will prove to be a journey, not a destination."

Dwight Eisenhower (34th U.S. President): "The present situation is to be regarded as one of opportunity for us and not of disaster."

John F. Kennedy (35th U.S. President): "Ask not what your country can do for you—ask what you can do for your country."

John F. Kennedy (35th U.S. President): "Let us resolve to be masters, not the victims, of our history."

Lyndon B. Johnson (36th U.S. President): "Our test before us . . . is not whether our commitments match our will and our courage; but whether we have the will and the courage to match our commitments."

Richard Nixon (37th U.S. President): "The ability to be cool, confident, and decisive in crisis . . . is the direct result of how well the individual has prepared himself for battle."

Gerald Ford (38th U.S. President): "Challenge and adversity have given us confidence and experience."

James Carter (39th U.S. President): "We must adjust to changing times and still hold to unchanging principles."

Ronald Reagan (40th U.S. President): "Wars begin when governments believe the price of aggression is cheap."

George H. W. Bush (41st U.S. President): "Strength in the pursuit of peace is no vice."

William Clinton (42nd U.S. President): "There can be no 'them' in America. There's only 'us.'"

"Warriors"

We all are warriors with sin. Crusading knights,
    we come to earth
With spotless plumes and shining shields to joust
    with foes and prove our worth.
The world is but a battlefield where strong and
    weak men fill the lists,
And some make war with humble prayers, and
    some with swords and some with fists.
And some for pleasure or for peace forsake their
    purposes and goals
And barter for the scarlet joys of ease and pomp,
Their knightly souls.

We're all enlisted soldiers here, in service for
    the term call life
And each of us in some grim way must bear his
    portion of the strife.
Temptations everywhere assail. Men do not rise
    by fearing sin,
Nor he who keeps within his tent, unharmed,
    unscratched, the crown shall win.
When wrongs are trampling mortals down and
    rank injustice stalks about,

Real manhood to the battle flies, and dies or puts
    the foes to rout.
'Tis not the new and shining blade that marks
    the soldier of the field,
His glory is his broken sword, his pride the
    scars upon his shield;
The crimson stains that sin has left upon his
    soul are tongues that speak
The victory of newfound strength by one who
    yesterday was weak.
And meaningless the spotless plume, the shining
    blade that goes through life
And quits this flaming battlefield without one
    evidence of strife.
We all are warriors with sin, we all are knights
    in life's crusades,
And with some form of tyranny, we're sent to
    earth to measure blades.
The courage of the soul must gleam in conflict
    with some fearful foe,
No man was ever born to life its luxuries
    alone to know.
And he who brothers with a sin to keep his
    outward garb unsoiled
And fears to battle with a wrong, shall find his
    soul decayed and spoiled.

A Word from Patriots

God grants liberty only to those who love it and are always ready to guard and defend it.

Daniel Webster

The inescapable price of liberty is an ability to preserve it from destruction.

Douglas MacArthur

Liberty is the proper end and object of authority, and cannot subsist without it; and it is a liberty to that only which is good, just, and honest.

John Winthrop

Those who would give up essential liberty to purchase a little temporary safety deserve neither liberty nor safety.

Benjamin Franklin

True liberty consists only in the power of doing what we ought to will, and in not being constrained to do what we ought not to will.

Jonathan Edwards

The tree of liberty must be refreshed from time to time with the blood of patriots and tyrants. It is its natural manure.

Thomas Jefferson

Let every nation know, whether it wishes us well or ill, that we shall pay any price, bear any burden, meet any hardship, support any friend, oppose any foe to assure the survival and the success of liberty.

John F. Kennedy

A Word from Patriots

He that would make his own liberty
secure must guard even his enemy
from oppression.

Thomas Paine

I would remind you that extremism in
the defense of liberty is no vice. And
let me remind you also that
moderation in the pursuit of justice is
no virtue.

Barry Goldwater

It is a common observation here that
our cause is the cause of all mankind,
and that we are fighting for their
liberty in defending our own.

Benjamin Franklin

Give me your tired, your poor, Your
huddled masses yearning to breathe
free, The wretched refuse of your
teeming shore; Send these, the
homeless, tempest-tossed to me. I lift
my lamp beside the golden door!

Emma Lazarus (found on the Statue of Liberty)

Our institutions of freedom will not survive unless they are constantly replenished by the faith that gave them birth.

John Foster Dulles

Those who expect to reap the blessings of freedom must, like men, undergo the fatigues of supporting it.

Thomas Paine

I intend no modification of my oft-expressed personal wish that all men everywhere could be free.

Abraham Lincoln

There can be no greater good than the quest for peace, and no finer purpose than the preservation of freedom.

Ronald Reagan

No man is entitled to the blessings of freedom unless he be vigilant in its preservation.

Douglas MacArthur

A Word from Patriots

*With malice toward none, with charity
for all, with firmness in the right, as
God gives us to see the right, let us
strive on to finish the work we are in,
to bind up the nation's wounds, to care
for him who shall have borne the
battle and for his widow and his
orphan, to do all which may achieve
and cherish a just and lasting peace
among ourselves and with all nations.*

Abraham Lincoln

*There is a just God who presides over
the destinies of nations and who will
raise up friends to fight our battles for
us. The battle, sir, is not to the strong
alone; it is to the vigilant, the active,
the brave. It is vain, sir, to extenuate
the matter. Gentlemen may cry, peace,
peace—but there is no peace. The war
is actually begun! The next gale that
sweeps from the north will bring to our
ears the clash of resounding arms!
Our brethren are already in the field!
Why stand we here idle? What is it
that gentlemen wish? What would they
have? Is life so dear, or peace so
sweet, as to be purchased at the price
of chains and slavery? Forbid it,
almighty God! I know not what course
others may take; but as for me, give
me liberty, or give me death!*

Patrick Henry

Eternal vigilance is the price of liberty; power is ever stealing from the many to the few.

The manna of popular liberty must be gathered each day, or it is rotten. The living sap of today outgrows the dead rind of yesterday. The hand entrusted with power becomes, either from human depravity or esprit de corps, the necessary enemy of the people. Only by continued oversight can the democrat in office be prevented from hardening into a despot; only by unintermitted agitation can a people be sufficiently awake to principle not to let liberty be smothered in material prosperity.

Wendell Phillips

If the fires of freedom and civil liberties burn low in other lands, they must be made brighter in our own. If in other lands, the press and books and literature of all kinds are censored, we must redouble our efforts here to keep them free. If in other lands the eternal truths of the past are threatened by intolerance, we must provide a safe place for their perpetuation.

Franklin D. Roosevelt

A Word from Patriots

It may be laid down as a primary position, and the basis of our system, that every citizen who enjoys the protection of a free government, owes not only a proportion of his property, but even his personal services to the defense of it, and consequently that the citizens of America (with a few legal and official exceptions) from eighteen to fifty years of age should be borne on the militia rolls, provided with uniform arms, and so far accustomed to the use of them, that the total strength of the country might be called forth at a short notice on a very interesting emergency.

George Washington

The sum of the whole matter is this, that our civilization cannot survive materially unless it be redeemed spiritually.

Woodrow Wilson

It is too probable that no plan we propose will be adopted. Perhaps another dreadful conflict is to be sustained. If to please the people, we offer what we ourselves disapprove, how can we afterwards defend our work? Let us raise a standard to which the wise and the honest can repair. The event is in the hand of God.

George Washington

A strong defense is the surest way to peace. Strength makes détente attainable. Weakness invites war. As my generation—my generation—knows from four very bitter experiences.

Gerald R. Ford

I have sworn upon the altar of God, eternal hostility against every form of tyranny over the mind of man.

Thomas Jefferson

SPIRIT OF LIBERTY

What is the spirit of liberty? I cannot define it; I can only tell you my own faith. The spirit of liberty is the spirit which is not too sure that it is right. The spirit of liberty is the spirit which seeks to understand the minds of other men and women. The spirit of liberty is the spirit which weighs their interests alongside its own without bias. The spirit of liberty remembers that not even a sparrow falls to the earth unheeded. The spirit of liberty is the spirit of Him who, nearly two thousand years ago, taught mankind that lesson it has never learned, but has never quite forgotten: that there may be a kingdom where the least shall be heard and considered side by side with the greatest.

Learned Hand

THE FOUR FREEDOMS

In the future days, which we seek to make secure, we look forward to a world founded upon four essential human freedoms.

The first is freedom of speech and expression—everywhere in the world.

The second is freedom of every person to worship God in his own way— everywhere in the world.

The third is freedom from want— which, translated into world terms, means economic understanding which will secure to every nation a healthy peacetime life for its inhabitants— everywhere in the world.

The fourth is freedom from fear— which, translated into world terms, means a worldwide reduction of armaments to such a fashion that no nation will be in a position to commit an act of physical aggression against any neighbor—anywhere in the world.

Franklin D. Roosevelt

DEDICATION

*I was born an American; I live an
American; I shall die an American; and
I intend to perform the duties
incumbent upon me in that character to
the end of my career. I mean to do this
with absolute disregard of personal
consequences. What are the personal
consequences? What is the individual
man, with all the good or evil that may
betide him, in comparison with the
good and evil which may befall a great
country, and in the midst of great
transactions which concern that
country's fate? Let the consequences be
what they will, I am careless. No man
can suffer too much, and no man can
fall too soon, if he suffer, or if he fall, in
the defense of the liberties and
constitution of his country.*

Daniel Webster

AMERICA'S GREATNESS

*I sought for the greatness and genius
of America in her commodious
harbors and her ample rivers, and it
was not there.*

*I sought for the greatness and genius
of America in her fertile fields and
boundless forests, and it was not there.*

*I sought for the greatness and genius of
America in her rich mines and her vast
world commerce, and it was not there.*

*I sought for the greatness and genius
of America in her public school system
and her institutions of learning, and it
was not there.*

*I sought for the greatness and genius
of America in her democratic congress
and her matchless constitution, and it
was not there.*

*Not until I went into the churches of
America and heard her pulpits flame
with righteousness did I understand
her genius and power.*

*America is great because America is
good, and if America ever ceases to be
good, America will cease to be great.*

Alexis de Tocqueville

A Time for Prayer

Our heartfelt prayers and sympathy go out to all who have been directly touched by this tragedy, and their families. I call upon all Americans to pray.

Rev. Billy Graham

America: Out of the Spiritual Ashes

In a land often accused of self-centeredness and self-indulgence, America proved she still had heart. The heart to choose life . . . in the midst of death. She chose life, she chose love, and in many cases, she chose self-sacrifice of the most immeasurable cost.

Amidst hijacked planes and fire-torn wreckage, the heart of Americans shone forth first through a flurry of cell phone rings and final messages of love. The strong beat of America continued as the survivors turned their attention to others, dragging their coworkers and sometimes strangers down the war-torn steps of evil to an unknown haven of safety. Some never made it, staggering up the stairs instead to give of themselves, to give their lives. In the aftermath, the heartbeat of America grew not fainter, but resoundingly stronger as innumerable volunteers clawed through the rubble, counseled the hurting, and gave blood for the wounded. America had chosen life for the living and sacrifice for the dying.

Finally, the heart of America gripped tightly and securely the faith of her fathers as she fell to her knees, weeping with the broken and praying for the shaken. "From whence shall my help come?" she asked, and her people answered, "God is our Refuge and Strength." Americans flocked to their churches and synagogues, their chapels and their mosques. Many went to give thanks for a life undeserved; others beckoned for comfort and healing in a time of bewilderment and loss. And yet, there were those who, in the still corridors of mourning, prayed for their enemies, the ones who had birthed an unimaginable disaster. Refusing to succumb to the hatred that permeated the debris, they reassured their Middle-Eastern neighbors of the United States that they would not be judged. America had chosen to love.

Like a wayward child floundering for a hand of guidance, America knew she had wandered too far. She had wandered too close to the brink of spiritual and physical death. But in the face of disaster, she knew where to go for comfort, healing, and protection. The heart of America had been immobilized for one brief moment—the once worthwhile became but a shadow to those who would forever be cherished. Nothing would ever be ordinary or normal again. America rose out of her spiritual ashes to her spiritual roots. And she remembered. Here within the walls of her churches was hope and the One who could sustain them through the worst catastrophe. Here was the One who could give them the energy to remain brave and the freedom to love . . . and they were right.

President George W. Bush's Address

National Day of Prayer and Remembrance
National Cathedral
Washington, D. C.
Friday, September 14, 2001

We are here in the middle hour of our grief. So many have suffered so great a loss, and today we express our nation's sorrow. We come before God to pray for the missing and the dead, and for those who loved them.

On Tuesday, our country was attacked with deliberate and massive cruelty. We have seen the images of fire and ashes and bent steel.

Now come the names, the list of casualties we are only beginning. They are the names of men and women who began their day at a desk or in an airport, busy with life. They are the names of people who faced death and in their last moments called home to say, 'Be brave' and 'I love you.'

They are the names of passengers who defied their murderers and prevented the murder of others on the ground. They are the names of men and women who wore the uniform of the United States and died at their posts.

They are the names of rescuers—the ones whom death found running up the stairs and into the fires to help others. We will read all these names. We will linger over them and learn their stories, and many Americans will weep.

To the children and parents and spouses and families and friends of the lost, we offer the deepest sympathy of the nation. And I assure you, you are not alone.

Just three days removed from these events, Americans do not yet have the distance of history, but our responsibility to history is already clear: to answer these attacks and rid the world of evil.

War has been waged against us by stealth and deceit and murder.

This nation is peaceful, but fierce when stirred to anger. This conflict was begun on the timing and terms of others; it will end in a way and at an hour of our choosing.

Our purpose as a nation is firm, yet our wounds as a people are recent and unhealed and lead us to pray. In many of our prayers this week, there's a searching and an honesty. At St. Patrick's Cathedral in New York, on Tuesday, a woman said, "I pray to God to give us a sign that He's still here."

Others have prayed for the same, searching hospital to hospital, carrying pictures of those still missing.

God's signs are not always the ones we look for. We learn in tragedy that His purposes are not always our own, yet the prayers of private suffering, whether in our homes or in this great cathedral are known and heard and understood.

There are prayers that help us last through the day or endure the night. There are prayers of friends and strangers that give us strength for the journey, and there are prayers that yield our will to a will greater than our own.

This world He created is of moral design. Grief and tragedy and hatred are only for a time. Goodness, remembrance, and love have no end, and the Lord of life holds all who die and all who mourn.

It is said that adversity introduces us to ourselves.

This is true of a nation as well. In this trial, we have been reminded and the world has seen that our fellow Americans are generous and kind, resourceful and brave.

We see our national character in rescuers working past exhaustion, in long lines of blood donors, in thousands of citizens who have asked to work and serve in any way possible. And we have seen our national character in eloquent acts of sacrifice. Inside the World Trade Center, one man who could have saved himself stayed until the end and at the side of his quadriplegic friend. A beloved priest died giving the last rites to a firefighter. Two office workers, finding a disabled stranger, carried her down sixty-eight floors to safety.

A group of men drove through the night from Dallas to Washington to bring skin grafts for burned victims. In these acts and many others, Americans showed a deep commitment to one another and an abiding love for our country.

Today, we feel what Franklin Roosevelt called "the warm courage of national unity." This is a unity of every faith and every background. This has joined together political parties and both houses of Congress. It is evident in services of prayer and candlelight vigils and American flags, which are displayed in pride and waved in defiance. Our unity is a kinship of grief and a steadfast resolve to prevail against our enemies. And this unity against terror is now extending across the world.

America is a nation full of good fortune, with so much to be grateful for, but we are not spared from suffering. In every generation, the world has produced enemies of human freedom. They have attacked America because we are freedom's home and defender, and the commitment of our fathers is now the calling of our time.

On this national day of prayer and remembrance, we ask Almighty God to watch over our nation and grant us patience and resolve in all that is to come. We pray that He will comfort and console those who now walk in sorrow. We thank Him for each life we now must mourn, and the promise of a life to come.

As we've been assured, "neither death nor life nor angels nor principalities, nor powers nor things present nor things to come nor height nor depth can separate us from God's love."

May He bless the souls of the departed. May He comfort our own. And may He always guide our country.

God bless America.

Prayer for Peace

Pope John Paul II
Astana, Kazakstan
Sunday, September 23, 2001

From this city, from Kazakstan, a country that is an example of harmony between men and women of different origins and beliefs, I wish to make an earnest call to everyone, Christians and the followers of other religions, that we work together to build a world without violence, a world that loves life, and grows in justice and solidarity. We must not let what has happened lead to a deepening of divisions. Religion must never be used as a reason for conflict.

From this place, I invite . . . God whose children we all are, that the supreme good of peace may reign in the world. May people everywhere, strengthened by divine wisdom, work for a civilization of love, in which there is no room for hatred, discrimination, or violence.

With all my heart, I beg God to keep the world in peace.

Amen.

"America, the Beautiful"

by Katherine L. Bates

O beautiful for spacious skies, For amber waves of grain,
For purple mountain majesties Above the fruited plain!
America! America! God shed His grace on thee,
And crown thy good with brotherhood From sea to
    shining sea!

O beautiful for pilgrim feet, Whose stern impassioned
    stress
A thoroughfare for freedom beat Across the wilderness!
America! America! God shed His grace on thee,
And crown thy good with brotherhood From sea to
    shining sea!

O beautiful for heroes proved In liberating strife.
Who more than self their country loved And mercy more
    than life!
America! America! May God thy gold refine
Till all success be nobleness And every gain divine!

O beautiful for patriot dream That sees beyond the years
Thine alabaster cities gleam Undimmed by human tears!
America! America! God shed His grace on thee,
And crown thy good with brotherhood From sea to
    shining sea!

God Returns to America's Public Square

By Janet Chismar

In the days following the September 11 attack on America, "pray" has become the rallying cry heard around the nation—and topics of religion and faith have surged front and center in the news. One Washington, D.C. commentator noted, "No one is asking for atheists they can interview on their talk shows," and Fox News reported Saturday, "We've seen a resurgence of public religion—Americans are rediscovering the power of faith."

Perhaps nothing so vividly symbolizes that public resurgence as when the members of Congress stood shoulder-to-shoulder and sang "God Bless America" on the Capitol steps.

Even secular newspapers are looking for prayers to print. *USA Today* will feature a full page ad tomorrow—"To help America speak to God with one voice: A Prayer by the Nation, For the Nation"—co-sponsored by the National Association of Evangelicals (NAE), America's National Prayer Committee, the National Day of Prayer Task Force, and the Mission America Coalition.

The NAE also urged its fifty-one member denominations and 43,000 churches to mobilize for a "National Day of Mourning and Prayer," on Sunday, Sept. 16. "Many people will look to churches, pastors, and people of faith for guidance and help," said Dr. Edward L. Foggs, NAE's chairman of the board. "The National Association of

Evangelicals encourages denominations, churches, and organizations to look to the Word of God for wisdom at this time and to be the people of God in the midst of tragedy."

Focus on the Family president James Dobson urged a national TV audience Friday to teach children to pray as a way of helping them learn to deal with the tragedy. He told CNN's Larry King: "Americans are very resilient. They have many resources, and two of the greatest are their families and their faith. And I believe that's where we will turn this time."

President George W. Bush set the tone at the government level when he designated September 14 a "National Day of Prayer and Remembrance," asking Americans to attend religious services of their choosing on their lunch hour and conduct candlelight prayer vigils in the evening.

Former Presidents Clinton, Bush, Carter, and Ford joined Bush at the Washington National Cathedral service Friday, which was broadcast nationally. "Our purpose as a nation is firm," said Bush. "Yet our wounds as a people are recent and unhealed, and lead us to pray.

"In many of our prayers this week, there is a searching, and an honesty," Bush continued. "At St. Patrick's Cathedral in New York on Tuesday, a woman said, 'I prayed to God to give us a sign that He is still here.' God's signs are not always the ones we look for. We learn in tragedy that His purposes are not always our own. Yet the prayers of private suffering, whether in our homes or in this great cathedral, are known and heard, and understood."

The Rev. Billy Graham told the congregation: "Today we come together in this service to confess our need of God. We've always needed God from the very beginning of time. But today we need Him especially."

Graham noted that the tragedy "can give a message of hope to the present and future. Yes, there is hope for the present because I believe the stage has already been set for a new spirit in our nation," he said. "One of the things we desperately need is a spiritual renewal in this country. We need a spiritual revival in America. God has told us in His Word time after time that if we repent of our sins and we turn to Him, He will bless us in a new way."

I believe the stage has already been set for a new spirit in our nation.

At the Pentagon, crowds of employees gathered for several ecumenical prayer services in memory of the victims of the terrorist attack. The service held at noon Friday in the Pentagon auditorium concluded with an overflow crowd of tearful employees singing "God Bless America."

Americans in all fifty states joined together Saturday for "America Prays," a vigil led by some of the nation's top pastors and speakers. Franklin Graham, James Dobson, Max Lucado, Bruce Wilkinson, and John Maxwell led the nation in prayer from Glad Tidings Church in Lake Charles, Louisiana.

The event was captured and sent via satellite to some 1,500 churches and broadcast on FamilyNet and Sky Angel; webcast on Crosswalk.com, and broadcast on radio through both the Salem and Moody networks.

Sunday church crowds rivaled those seen on Christmas, a fact reported by most major news organizations. In the center of Manhattan, in Washington's suburbs, and across the heartland of America, sanctuaries filled with overflow crowds.

According to the *Washington Post,* some people said they had taken "an unfamiliar step into a church to feel a solidarity with their fellow bereaved citizens," while others said they'd come for healing and to pray for the dead.

The two morning services at the Washington National Cathedral drew about 7,000 people of all faiths, with hundreds more listening to the sermon on loudspeakers in the plaza outside. Sunday services normally draw about 1,500 people, a cathedral spokesman said.

Fox News reports that at St. Ignatius Loyola Catholic Church on New York City's Upper East Side, firefighters from the East 85th Street station carried bread and wine to the altar for communion. The fire brigade at East 85th Street was one of the early crews on the scene, and has one known fatality plus nine others missing. Afterwards, as they somberly walked back down the aisle to leave, the congregation bid them farewell for several minutes with an emotional standing ovation. Parishioners sobbed.

But some pastors conducted "business as usual." Rod Stafford, senior pastor of Fairfax Community Church in suburban Virginia, said he did not need to prepare a special sermon.

"On any given Sunday," explained Stafford, "no matter what is going on, the church has something relevant to say. We don't need to change our message on the basis of world events."

While the terrorists may have intended to bring America to its knees, perhaps they did not realize how fitting an analogy that would be. It has driven the nation to prayer. As Billy Graham said, "Those perpetrators who took this on to tear us apart, it has worked the other way."

"Prophecy"

We shall thank our God for graces
That we've never known before;
We shall look on manlier faces
When our troubled days are o'er.
We shall rise a better nation
From the battle's grief and grime
And shall win our soul's salvation
In this bitter trial time.
And the old Flag waving o'er us
In the dancing morning sun
Will be daily singing for us
Of a splendor new begun.
When the rifles cease to rattle
And the cannon cease to roar,
When is passed the smoke of battle
And the death lists are no more,
With a yet undreamed of beauty
As a people we shall rise,
And a love of right and duty
Shall be gleaming in our eyes.
As a country, tried by sorrow,
With a heritage of worth,
We shall stand in that tomorrow
With the leaders of the earth.

*America was founded by people who
[believed] that God was their Rock of
safety. I recognize we must be
cautious in claiming that God is on
our side, but I think it's all right to
keep asking if we're on His side.*

Ronald Reagan,
40th U.S. President

"America"

Samuel F. Smith

My country 'tis of thee, Sweet land of liberty,
Of thee I sing: Land where my fathers died, Land of
the pilgrim's pride, From every mountainside Let
freedom ring!

My native country, thee, Land of the noble free,
Thy name I love: I love thy rocks and rills, Thy woods
and templed hills; My heart with rapture thrills Like
that above.

Let music swell the breeze, And ring from all the trees
Sweet freedom's song: Let mortal tongues awake; Let all
that breathe partake; Let rocks their silence break,
The sound prolong.

Our fathers' God, to Thee, Author of liberty,
To Thee we sing: Long may our land be bright With
freedom's holy light; Protect us by Thy might, Great
God, our King!

Where Is God?

By Brenda Ropoulos

Talk about opportunities to practice one's godliness. One man wailed to a woman, "Where is God? Where is God?" It was obvious to me, as it was to her . . . she was late for work and was just entering the building . . . that God was truly everywhere. I have never seen so many people come together to do whatever it took to help one another. It took me nearly 8 hours to get to my sister (I was two blocks away, at the New York Stock Exchange, which people feared would be the next target when it all happened). The entire situation was beyond eerie. I wore another's shoes, was directed to safe transportation by the NYPD, carried across the river by the crew of a sugar boat who had volunteered to help the Coast Guard, was met by the Army Corps of Engineers who put us on a bus to take us to a Path train to get me onto a train to come north. I shared food and drink with those who had none, and have never hugged or rubbed or held hands with so many wonderful people in my life. Hand written signs on 8 1/2 x 11 paper stuck on street lights told people where they could go to get out. I left everything I had in my hotel room in midtown. I would have had to have walked 55 blocks up and 55 blocks back to be able to get across the river again . . . it really seemed pointless. Thank you, thank you, thank you for all your prayers. I felt so close all day.

The Firefighters Prayer

When duty call's me, oh Lord, my partner,
When flames do their destructive work,
Give me strength to save lives
And, above all, keep my courage bright.

With you will I reach, before it's too late,
The injured child, the helpless old person,
With your generosity, may I be able
To spare them the horror of such an end.

Since I must always be alert,
I pray thee, oh Lord, guide me every move,
And in the infernal tumult of the fire
Let me hear the feeblest cry.

I will glory in the fulfillment of my destiny,
For is not life-saving the most noble calling?
When the storm is over and all have returned home,
Then will I be proud to have helped my neighbor

If it should happen, by thy will,
That I must give my life,
I pray thee, protect my family
And bless this firefighter who is yours.

Do It Again, Lord

By Max Lucado

Dear Lord,

We're still hoping we'll wake up. We're still hoping we'll open a sleepy eye and think, "What a horrible dream."

But we won't, will we, Father? What we saw was not a dream. Planes did gouge towers. Flames did consume our fortress. People did perish. It was no dream and, dear Father, we are sad.

There is a ballet dancer who will no longer dance and a doctor who will no longer heal. A church has lost her priest; a classroom is minus a teacher. Cora ran a food pantry. Paige was a counselor, and Dana, dearest Father, Dana was only three years old. (Who held her in those final moments?)

We are sad, Father. For as the innocent are buried, our innocence is buried as well. We thought we were safe. Perhaps we should have known better. But we didn't.

And so we come to You. We don't ask You for help; we beg You for it. We don't request it; we implore it. We know what You can do. We've read the accounts. We've pondered the stories and now we plead, Do it again, Lord. Do it again.

Remember Joseph? You rescued him from the pit. You can do the same for us. Do it again, Lord.

Remember the Hebrews in Egypt? You protected their children from the angel of death. We have children, too, Lord. Do it again.

And Sarah? Remember her prayers? You heard them. Joshua? Remember his fears? You inspired him. The women at the tomb? You resurrected their hope. The doubts of Thomas? You took them away. Do it again, Lord. Do it again.

You changed Daniel from a captive into a king's counselor. You took Peter the fisherman and made him Peter an apostle. Because of You, David went from leading sheep to leading armies. Do it again, Lord, for we need counselors today, Lord. We need apostles. We need leaders. Do it again, dear Lord.

Most of all, do again what you did at Calvary. What we saw here on that Tuesday, you saw there on that Friday. Innocence slaughtered. Goodness murdered. Mothers weeping. Evil dancing. Just as the ash fell on our children, the darkness fell on your Son. Just as our towers were shattered, the very Tower of Eternity was pierced.

And by dusk, heaven's sweetest song was silent, buried behind a rock.

But You did not waver, O Lord. You did not waver. After three days in a dark hole, You rolled the rock and rumbled the earth and turned the darkest Friday into the brightest Sunday. Do it again, Lord. Grant us a September Easter.

We thank You, dear Father, for these hours of unity. Disaster has done what discussion could not. Doctrinal fences have fallen. Republicans are standing with Democrats.

Skin colors have been covered by the ash of burning buildings. We thank You for these hours of unity.

And we thank You for these hours of prayer. The Enemy sought to bring us to our knees and succeeded. He had no idea, however, that we would kneel before You. And he has no idea what You can do.

Let Your mercy be upon our president, vice president, and their families. Grant to those who lead us wisdom beyond their years and experience. Have mercy upon the souls who have departed and the wounded who remain. Give us grace that we might forgive and faith that we might believe.

And look kindly upon Your church. For two thousand years You've used her to heal a hurting world.

Do it again, Lord. Do it again.

Through Christ, Amen.

Written by Max Lucado for America Prays, a national prayer vigil held Saturday, September 14, 2001. Reprinted with permission.

Lincoln's Prayer Proclamation

On March 30, 1863, President Abraham Lincoln issued an historic prclamation appointing a National Day of Prayer and Fasting:

Whereas, the Senate of the United States, devoutly recognizing the supreme authority and just government of the Almighty God in all the affairs of men and of nations has by a resolution requested the president to designate and set apart a day for national prayer and humiliation.

And whereas, it is the duty of nations as well as of men to own their dependence upon the overruling power of God: to confess their sins and transgressions in humble sorrow, yet with assured hope that genuine repentance will lead to mercy and pardon: and to recognize the sublime truth, announced in the Holy Scriptures and proven by all history that those nations only are blessed who God is the Lord:

And insomuch as we know that by His divine law nations, like individuals, are subjected to punishments and chastisements in this world, may we not justly fear that the awful calamity of civil war which now desolates the land may be but a punishment inflicted upon us for our presumptuous sins, to the needful end of our national reformation as a whole people? We have been the recipients of the choicest bounties of Heaven. We have been preserved, these many years, in peace and prosperity. We have grown in numbers, wealth, and power as no other nation has ever grown; but we have forgotten God. We have forgotten the gracious land, which preserved us in peace, and multiplied and enriched and strengthened us; and we have vainly imagined in the deceitfulness of our hearts, that all these blessings were produced by some superior wisdom and virtue of our own. Intoxicated with unbroken success, we have become too self-sufficient to feel the necessity of redeeming and preserving grace, too proud to pray to the God who made us.

It behooves us then, to humble ourselves before the offended Power, to confess our national sins, and to pray for clemency and forgiveness.

All this being done in sincerity and truth, let us then rest humbly in the hope authorized by the divine teachings, that the united cry of the nation will be heard on high, and answered with blessings no less than the pardon of our national sins, and the restoration of our now divided and suffering country to its former happy condition of unity and peace.

Abraham Lincoln

Psalm 46 TLB

GOD IS OUR refuge and strength, a tested help in times of trouble. And so we need not fear even if the world blows up, and the mountains crumble into the sea. Let the oceans roar and foam; let the mountains tremble!

There is a river of joy flowing through the City of our God—the sacred home of the God above all gods. God himself is living in that City; therefore it stands unmoved despite the turmoil everywhere. He will not delay his help. The nations rant and rave in anger—but when God speaks, the earth melts in submission and kingdoms totter into ruin.

The Commander of the armies of heaven is here among us. He, the God of Jacob, has come to rescue us. Come, see the glorious things that our God does, how he brings ruin upon the world, and causes wars to end throughout the earth, breaking and burning every weapon. "Stand Silent! Know that I am God! I will be honored by every nation in the world!"

The Commander of the heavenly armies is here among *us!* He, the God of Jacob, has come to rescue *us!*

There are a good many problems before the American people today, and before me as President, but I expect to find the solution to those problems just in the proportion that I am faithful in the study of the Word of God.

Woodrow Wilson,
28th U.S. President

Notes from the Rubble

By Seth Castleman

The first moment to write and the hands not yet steady on the keyboard. I hope I have not added to anyone's worry, by not checking in sooner. I am alive and physically unhurt. I was ironing a shirt to leave for an errand at Park Place when I got the call about the disaster Tuesday morning. Park Place, I have been told, was crushed by part of the falling buildings. Since midday Tuesday, I have been mostly at the sight helping with relief efforts.

The world is a whirl of love and sorrow. What follows may be well short of organized and only bordering on coherent, but considering the state of things, perhaps it is appropriate. I wanted to share some experiences, to help let them go, and to bring more people together in the communal suffering and supporting.

First . . . the despair and frustration and sorrow and fear that we are all feeling. The helplessness. We all wish we could just get our hands on something to do. I do not know how you can help, other than to pray and bear witness. You have likely seen news more than I have over these days, so I cannot tell people how to offer support. I do not know if this is still the case, as I have been home for the last twelve hours getting some sleep, but for the two days prior we were having to turn away many volunteers. So much good will and so little that we can do.

The volunteer effort of thousands, while very disorganized with right and left often unaware of the other, is in very good spirits with great depths of kindness and strength. I have fallen in love and made dozens of dear friends, as the best in people shines through in such times.

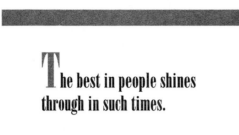

T he best in people shines through in such times.

I have spent most of these days at Chelsea Piers, coordinating the crisis unit for families looking for loved ones, and then at Ground Zero amidst rubble and dust and shocked, sullen faces doing chaplaincy and crisis counseling and coordinating counseling for the rescue workers. People come in to the Chelsea Pier unit after visiting every hospital in the city, desperate for some news. The volunteer counselors and chaplains fill out missing persons reports, sit with them, look at photos together, weep, laugh, sit in silence. We give out hospital phone numbers, let them see lists of the confirmed safe, enter all the data and scan photos for a FEMA database of missing persons. We hold hands and counsel and encourage people perhaps to go home and be together with loved ones, as there is little else to do. The waiting and not knowing is the most difficult part. Not sure whether to hope or mourn, the families feel helpless and overwhelmed with fear.

At Ground Zero, there is equal helplessness. We are counseling firefighters, EMTs, iron workers, and police as they come out of the rubble. For the families it is horrible not to know, for these guys it is horrible to know.

I talked with no one who had found a body. Only parts. Masses of pieces. Collecting fingers by the hundreds, finger printing them and throwing them into bags, sorting by size. Pediatrics here, adults here. . . . An army man in post traumatic stress, weeping about scooping up guts, about reaching into crevasses to grasp a hand, only a hand.

How devastating to return to the family crisis unit after spending all night hearing these stories from the men in the rubble. And God, as if to say, 'Do not take this to mean that The Presence is not here,' appeared in moments and miracles.

A firefighter from upstate who I sat with for an hour next to the rubble. He found a body of a young Asian man, flattened to just a few inches. The form was covered in another inch or two of dust. (There are no cement blocks to move, as all the cement and sheet rock crumbled to a fine and asbestos-filled dust which covers the ground and fills the air.) The body was almost invisible under the dust, yet in the beam of his light, something shone. The left hand was grey like everything else, but on one finger was a gold wedding band, uncovered and shining clean, a golden line in a sea of deathly grey. We mused together whether another worker had been there first and cleaned it off and if so why he hadn't collected the body or if an angel had passed by.

Shannon, a small retriever dog, sniffed and saved five people at the Pentagon, then came here to find another four. At least ten dogs have been killed in the wreckage. They dig when they smell a human life, lie down when they smell a dead body. Almost no barks, and lying down is easier and easier as the smell turns to stench.

My tag says *chaplain,* so people come up to talk, pray, breathe, or just be silent together. I am struck how much The Presence (as God is sometimes called) can so be found in the presence held between two people.

In the notebook I am using for volunteer names and numbers and random details, I came across a note to myself that I wrote on Sunday night before the disaster. In the Holocaust, no one was there to bear witness. People either oppressed or were oppressed, helped or turned their eyes away. What would happen if people opened their hearts and truly watched in Jerusalem? Can we deeply accept tragedy with an open heart, then move to heal and help from the seat of witness? The atoms that change when watched become the world that has been transformed.

At Ground Zero, amidst all the togetherness and kindness and effort, there are still thoughts and talk of those who planned this disaster. It is strange. I can only imagine the motives of those who committed these acts. Undoubtedly, they were frustrated, hurt. Undoubtedly, they felt politically, economically, culturally, and individually helpless, frustrated, afraid, and angry. These feelings are universal, the world filled with sorrow. The rescue workers, the families, the world, all feeling helpless, afraid, frustrated, and angry with this disaster. What motivates the killer so, too, inspires the healers. The actions so profoundly different; the initial spark perhaps the same.

I don't know if I am making this clear, but it feels so important. Will the heart open or close? Will we take our sadness and let it harden or let it melt? Do we allow it to turn to hatred or to love? They say the heart cannot fully love until it is broken; only the shattered vessel can hold water.

So, too, only a broken heart can harden into hatred. Only shattered shards become boxcutters and knives.

How easily these feelings can turn! Food that one day can nourish us and save our lives, turns rancid and kills. Love and hatred, good and evil, they seem so far apart, but no farther than water is from ice, and ice from turning back to water.

The Atrium, filled with palm trees in the Amex Building at the World Trade Center, where chamber orchestras once played, now is eerily silent. The banners are faded of their writing, ripped and dangling like sails of a pirate ship found on a deserted island. Tangled steel cuts the view of sky through shattered portals. And through the dust and smoke and sounds of slogging feet through water, comes the yellow slice of moon. Only she, it seems is consistent.

Later, just before dawn, she has ascended above the cloud. So much devastation, the earth and the psyche marred with death and still a beautiful new moon, rising white and untouched above our sorrow.

> *We all can pray. We all should pray.*
> *We should ask the fulfillment of God's*
> *will. We should ask for courage,*
> *wisdom, for the quietness of soul*
> *which comes alone to them who place*
> *their lives in His hands.*

Harry S Truman,
33rd U.S. President

Psalm 23 NASB

THE LORD is my shepherd, I shall not want.

He makes me lie down in green pastures;
He leads me beside quiet waters.

He restores my soul; He guides me in the
paths of righteousness For His name's sake.

Even though I walk through the valley of
the shadow of death, I fear no evil; for
Thou art with me; Thy rod and Thy staff,
they comfort me.

Thou dost prepare a table before me in the
presence of my enemies; Thou hast
anointed my head with oil; My cup
overflows.

Surely goodness and lovingkindness will
follow me all the days of my life, And I
will dwell in the house of the LORD forever.

Tonight I ask for your prayers for all
those who grieve, for the children
whose worlds have been shattered, for
all whose sense of safety and security
has been threatened. And I pray they
will be comforted by a Power greater
than any of us. Spoken through the
ages in Psalm 23: "Even though I
walk through the valley of the shadow
of death, I fear no evil, for you are
with me."

President George W. Bush addressing the nation on the
evening of September 11, 2001

A Prayer for Our Military

Thank You, Lord, for the men and women of our armed forces. Protect them as they protect us. Defend them as they defend us. Encourage and strengthen their spirits, souls, and bodies in the execution of their duties and responsibilities. May they be mentally and physically strong when required to face the challenges of combat. Undergird them with Your spirit and might when they are called upon to endure the hardships of battle.

I pray that nothing would take them by surprise but that they would be aware of all potential aggression. Enable them to curtail hostile actions before they start.

Reveal to our military leaders the strategies and plots that enemies would wage. Give our leaders wisdom and insight in all decisions. May response to any aggression by enemies of this nation be swift, accurate, and effective.

Father, give our military favor with the governmental agencies of this country. I pray that our Congress would appropriate sufficient funds to keep our nation's military preeminent in the world. Thank You, Lord, for providing America with the best-trained, equipped, and superior military force in the world today. Fill them with Your saving grace and the Gospel of peace that they may be shining witnesses of Your love.

Scripture References
Matthew 9:37-38
Romans 10:13-15
Psalms 119:114,117
Isaiah 41:12-13

Religious faith has the miraculous power to lift ordinary human beings to greatness in seasons of stress.

—Sam J. Ervin Jr., NBA player for the Seattle Supersonics

Decisions in National Crisis

Father God, in the name of Jesus, I pray that You would direct the leaders of this nation in times of crisis. Grant them wisdom and understanding, and help them to respond quickly and effectively to each situation. May divinely directed decisions be on their lips, and may they do that which is right in Your sight. May they follow Your will to direct our nation in the paths of peace and safety.

Unite all response agencies in an organized and harmonious fashion to bring quick and effective resolve to the demands of this crisis.

Empower us as United States citizens to do our part, financially, physically, emotionally, and spiritually, to support all who have been affected by this tragedy.

I pray that You encourage and strengthen our nation. Surround us with Your love and mercy. Bring peace and comfort to all those who are suffering as a result of this crisis.

Scripture References
Proverbs 16:10 AMP
Proverbs 11:3-6

Renewing our knowledge of and faith in God through Holy Scripture can strengthen us as a nation and a people.

—The Year of the Bible was declared in 1983 by a joint resolution of the House and Senate.

The Families of Our Military

Father, in the name of the Lord Jesus, I also lift up to You in prayer the families of our military. I pray that the Gospel will extend to them, that they might know Him and the power of His resurrection.

Father, I desire that these families might be a prayer force for our nation and our military.

May they know abundance and no lack. May they be well provided for and well taken care of.

Father, give them the courage of warriors. May the peace that passes understanding sustain them in seasons of separation.

Comfort them with Your Word, that they might have faith to see their sons, daughters, husbands, and wives returned to them in wholeness and safety.

Scripture References
Matthew 9:37-38
Philippians 4:7
Philippians 3:10
2 Corinthians 1:3-4

With a good conscience our only sure reward, with history the final judge of our deeds, let us go forth to lead the land we love, asking His blessing and His help, but knowing that here on earth God's work must truly be our own.

—John F. Kennedy, 35th U.S. President

National Protection

Most High God, I come to You in the name of Jesus, asking for divine protection for the people of this nation. I pray for the safety of every man, woman, and child. Keep us from harm's way, and provide protection from plans of destruction that our enemies have plotted. Stop strategies of destruction that our enemies would try to evoke.

Give wisdom, understanding, and discernment to those who provide protection. Help us to be watchful and alert to signs of wrongdoing.

Provide insight to national and local authorities on ways to guard, defend, and insure the safety of all American citizens both at home and abroad. Help us to unite with government leaders and law enforcement personnel in making this country a safe place to live, work, and play; allowing Americans to enjoy freedom without fear.

Scripture References
John 16:13
Romans 8:14
Matthew 18:19-20

Our prayer and God's mercy are like two buckets in a well; while the one ascends the other descends.

—Mary Hopkins, U.S. educator

Protection from Terrorism

Almighty God, I pray that You prevent the destructive forces of terrorism directed against our nation. Provide protection from evil attacks and stop the aggressors that attempt to bring destruction to our nation and people. May Your hand of protection keep us safe.

I stand against the spirit of fear that accompanies the cowardice acts of terrorism. Allow our fear to turn to trust in You. May knowledge of terrorist-planned attacks be revealed to those who provide our national and international security. Help those in power to act swiftly to avert all danger, protecting American lives and property.

Provide strength, courage, and wisdom to the protectors of this nation to administer their duties. Give wisdom and insight to our government and everyone involved in the elimination of terrorism. Provide instruction in the development of effective and efficient anti-terrorist strategies that will give us an advantage against our aggressors, allowing the country to remain safe and secure.

I pray that the instigators of terroism recognize the evil of their ways and repent and denounce their cowardice acts of destruction against humanity. Without repentance, may they reap the consequences of their actions, and may the fear of our retaliation be greater than their hatred of democracy.

Guide us in efforts to seek out and eradicate these merchants of death. Reveal the names of those responsible and those who are in allegiance with terrorist organizations to our authorities. Enable the military to become swift, powerful, and accurate in any action of retaliation.

Lord, help us to understand lifestyle changes that might be necessary to ensure our protection. Grant patience and tolerance to us in adapting to the safety precautions and measures that we might experience. Enable us to realize that the cost of inconvenience is a small price to pay for the safety of our families and of our nation.

Scripture References
Deuteronomy 29:29
Psalms 91:1-6
Daniel 11:25
Deuteronomy 31:6
Psalm 27:14

The spirit of man is more important than mere physical strength, and the spiritual fiber of a nation than its wealth.

—Dwight D. Eisenhower, 34th U.S. President

Ephesians 6:10-18 NLT

Be strong with the Lord's mighty power. Put on all of God's armor so that you will be able to stand firm against all strategies and tricks of the Devil. For we are not fighting against people made of flesh and blood, but against the evil rulers and authorities of the unseen world, against those mighty powers of darkness who rule this world, and against wicked spirits in the heavenly realms.

Use every piece of God's armor to resist the enemy in the time of evil, so that after the battle you will still be standing firm. Stand your ground, putting on the sturdy belt of truth and the body armor of God's righteousness. For shoes, put on the peace that comes from the Good News, so that you will be fully prepared. In every battle you will need faith as your shield to stop the fiery arrows aimed at you by Satan. Put on salvation as your helmet, and take the sword of the Spirit, which is the word of God. Pray at all times and on every occasion in the power of the Holy Spirit. Stay alert and be persistent in your prayers for all Christians everywhere.

In Time of War

Father, I come to You, in the name of our Lord Jesus, to lift up in prayer this present military action. Father, I pray that there might be a quick resolution to this action and that truth and righteousness would prevail.

May You guide, bless, and protect all those engaged in this conflict. Heal the physical and spiritual wounds that they may be inflicted.

Father, the gospel of the kingdom must be preached to this nation. I pray that what Satan has intended and devised to hinder the gospel You will turn to our good, that the gospel will go into this nation unimpeded.

Let all who hear Your Word turn to You for guidance, courage, and hope.

Scripture References
1 Timothy 2:1-4
Matthew 24:14
Genesis 50:20

God presides over the destinies of nations.

Patrick Henry

A Prayer for America

By the National Prayer Committee

Father, once again we are reminded that any security we have as individuals and as a nation comes only from the abiding hope and trust we have in You. Once again, we are cut to the heart at the loss of life and damage to peace that we have suffered as a nation.

So, Father, today we come to you and we seek Your peace for the families and victims of the horrible tragedy. For those still lost in the rubble of the destruction, we ask for the safety of Your hand. For those consumed by worry and fear as they try to locate missing loved ones, we ask for the comforting presence of Your spirit.

We seek Your peace for the emergency workers—that You would guard their lives as they seek to guard the lives of others. Give them the wisdom they need to perform their duties above and beyond the levels of their training.

And Father, we seek Your peace for our nation and our world. In the midst of our questions and uncertainty, we recognize that the unknown details of this day are already in Your grasp. We know You sent Your Son as the Prince of Peace, and even this day we fall under His command. Help us to find the strength and comfort we need as a nation to continue to humble ourselves, pray, and seek Your face for a new day in America and a new hope for our world.

> *Be joyful in hope, patient in affliction, faithful in prayer.*
>
> —Romans 12:12

The Lord's Prayer

"Pray, then, in this way: 'Our Father who art in heaven, Hallowed be Thy name.

'Thy kingdom come. Thy will be done, On earth as it is in heaven.

'Give us this day our daily bread.

'And forgive us our debts, as we also have forgiven our debtors.

'And do not lead us into temptation, but deliver us from evil. [For Thine is the kingdom, and the power, and the glory forever. Amen.]'

"For if you forgive men for their transgressions, your heavenly Father will also forgive you.

"But if you do not forgive men, then your Father will not forgive your transgressions."

Matthew 6:9-15 NASB

Right now God has brought this country to its knees. But let whosoever shall rise against this nation understand that we have not dropped to our knees because we are defeated, but we have dropped to our knees because we are armed and dangerous and ready to fight the good fight of faith.

—Bishop T. D. Jakes, Pastor of Potter's House Church, Dallas, Texas

A Prayer for Our Armed Forces

Dear Lord,

We thank you for the freedom we enjoy. That freedom, however, didn't come without a price. Just as You sacrificed for our eternal freedom, our forefathers gave their lives for our national freedom. May our military, which is under You, be able to understand the cause that they defend and that is at stake every time they don their military uniforms. Bless them, increase their territory, have Your hand on them, and keep them from evil and harm.

In times of war help our troops trust You, their leaders, their comrades, and themselves. May their accuracy be with full precision and excellence. May You preserve life supernaturally. As it says in the Bible, "Vengeance is mine sayeth the Lord," so help each member to not take vengeance into his or her own hands, but instead, to trust that Your justice will be sufficient.

Lord, because we are a free country we have many enemies—known and unknown. So Father, we ask that You uncover them and the secrecy and the lies. Let the fear of the Lord fall on them, and may they find their fate. For we know that it is not by our might or power, but by Your Spirit that we win.

Be with each family that is represented behind each uniform, whether their loved one is defending at home or abroad. Bring peace and rest to the family members, and as it says in Proverbs 3:5-6, help them to trust in You with all their hearts and lean not on their own understanding. Remind them that if they will acknowledge You in all their ways, You will make their paths straight.

Protect and bless our president in his efforts to lead our military. Help him and his leadership to keenly construct a strategy that will help to keep our forces fully trained and ready for any type of task that is requested of them. May You lead him in all decisions that he needs to make.

Lord, thank You for our Allies. Bless each nation and their people.

In Jesus' Name, Amen.

By Andy Fraser

Scripture on Protection

Psalm 91 NASB

HE who dwells in the shelter of the Most High Will abide in the shadow of the Almighty.

I will say to the LORD, "My refuge and my fortress, My God, in whom I trust!"

For it is He who delivers you from the snare of the trapper, And from the deadly pestilence.

He will cover you with His pinions, And under His wings you may seek refuge; His faithfulness is a shield and bulwark.

You will not be afraid of the terror by night, Or of the arrow that flies by day;

Of the pestilence that stalks in darkness, Or of the destruction that lays waste at noon.

A thousand may fall at your side, And ten thousand at your right hand; *But* it shall not approach you.

You will only look on with your eyes, And see the recompense of the wicked.

For you have made the LORD, my refuge, *Even* the Most High, your dwelling place.

No evil will befall you, Nor will any plague come near your tent.

For He will give His angels charge concerning you, To guard you in all your ways.

They will bear you up in their hands, Lest you strike your foot against a stone.

You will tread upon the lion and cobra, The young lion and the serpent you will trample down.

"Because he has loved Me, therefore I will deliver him; I will set him *securely* on high, because he has known My name.

"He will call upon Me, and I will answer him; I will be with him in trouble; I will rescue him, and honor him.

"With a long life I will satisfy him, And let him behold My salvation."

My Prayer to Jesus

Dear Heavenly Father,

I pray for our country. I pray for our president. Please give him Your wisdom. Help our country be united. Give our people Your peace, Lord. I pray that people's hearts will be softened and they will turn to You. I pray terrorism will be defeated and destroyed. Give our military and our people strength to overcome this battle against terrorism. I love You, Jesus. In Your name I pray, Amen.

Michelle, age 12
Tulsa, Oklahoma

"Battle Hymn of the Republic"

Julia W. Howe

Mine eyes have seen the glory of the coming of the Lord;
He is trampling out the vintage where the grapes of wrath are
stored;
He hath loosed the fateful lightning of his terrible swift sword;
His truth is marching on. Glory! Glory, hallelujah! Glory! Glory,
hallelujah! Glory! Glory, hallelujah! His truth is marching on.

I have seen Him in the watchfires of a hundred circling camps;
They have builded Him an altar in the evening dews and damps;
I can read his righteous sentence by the dim and flaring lamps;
Our God is marching on. Glory! Glory, hallelujah! Glory! Glory,
hallelujah! Glory! Glory, hallelujah! His day is marching on.

He has sounded forth the trumpet that shall never sound
retreat;
He is sifting out the hearts of men before his judgment seat,
O be swift, my soul, to answer Him! Be jubilant, my feet!
Our God is marching on. Glory! Glory, hallelujah! Glory! Glory,
hallelujah! Glory! Glory, hallelujah! Our God is marching on.

In the beauty of the lilies Christ was born across the sea,
With a glory in His bosom that transfigures you and me;
As he died to make men holy, let us die to make men free;
While God is marching on. Glory! Glory, hallelujah! Glory!
Glory, hallelujah! Glory! Glory, hallelujah! While God is
marching on.

A Month of Prayers for Our Nation

Day 1

Whoever acknowledges me before men, I will also acknowledge him before my father. Matthew 10:32

Dear Lord,

We thank You for the faith of our forefathers, for their desire to see this country grow in commitment to You. Help us to honor their prayers by turning to You and seeking Your counsel, that we might acknowledge You before all nations. Amen

Day 2

Blessed are the poor in spirit, for theirs is the kingdom of heaven. Mathew 5:3

Dear Lord,

We lift to You the lonely in heart, those captive to the quiet of their homes. Let us reach out to one another with Christ's love and willingly offer them companionship and solace. Amen

Day 3

Make level paths for your feet and take only ways that are firm. Proverbs 4:26

Dear Father,

You have given us the capacity to create and invent. Help us to use these gifts wisely, for the advancement of Your purposes in this land. Teach us discernment, that we may not abuse Your creativity under the guise of a greater good. Amen

Day 4

Praise the Lord, O my soul. Psalm 104:1

Dear Lord,

You have been gracious in allowing us the freedom to worship in this united land. Help us to take full advantage of that freedom, worshiping you often, without reservation. Fill our hearts with love for You and help us to express that feeling in daily devotion. Remind us Father, not to take this gift for granted. Amen

Day 5

As it is, there are many parts, but one body.

1 Corinthians 12:20

Dear Lord,

We thank you for the vast differences in the people you have created. Help us to recognize the gift each culture offers to this nation. We ask Your forgiveness for our own intolerance and plead for Your help in repairing the torn fabric of our nations cultural tapestry. Amen

Day 6

I looked for a man among them who would build up the wall and stand before me in the gap, on behalf of the land.

Ezekial 22:30

Dear Father,

Please bless our president. Open his eyes and ears to Your presence that he might guide us in a manner pleasing to You. Give him courage, strength, and wisdom to fight worldly perspectives and uphold all that is pure and honorable. Amen

Day 7

Let us therefore make every effort to do what leads to peace and to mutual edification.   Romans 14:19

Dear Lord,

We thank You for the Pastors of this nation. Thank You for their insight and willingness to serve. Please bless them Lord, that they might speak Your truth, shepherd Your children and know Your replenishment and peace. Amen

Day 8

Contend O Lord with those who contend with me, fight against those who fight against me.   Psalms 35:1

Dear Father,

We thank You for the men and women in the Army, for their willing commitment to protect our country from harm. Grant them courage and peace, help them to rely on You in the wilderness, and guide them safely home again. Amen

Day 9

Love your neighbor as yourself. Leviticus 19:18

Thank You Lord for community... for towns, cities and neighborhoods. Keep us from tucking within ourselves and help us to reach out to one another as You have reached out to us. Forgive us our habit of keeping to ourselves and let us open our homes and extend Your hospitality. Amen

Day 10

God blessed them and said be fruitful and increase in number.

Genesis 1:22

Dear Lord,

We thank You for the gift of life, for allowing generation to follow generation. Forgive us for our casual indifference to participating in such a miracle. Help us to honor the process of life's beginning, that we might see it as the true and genuine gift You intended it to be. Amen

Day 11

For since the creation of the world, God's invisible qualities... have been clearly seen, being understood from what has been made. Romans 1:20

Thank you for the beauty of creation, for the diversity this country offers. In snow-capped mountains and quiet pastures we see the evidence of Your mighty hand. We thank You for such a tangible reality of Your existence. . . forgive us for our unwillingness to see and open our eyes to the majesty of Your works. Amen

Day 12

Then he climbed into the boat with them, and the wind died down... they were completely amazed. Mark 6:51

Dear Father,

We thank You for the men and women who serve our country at sea. Grant them safe passage as they seek to protect and fortify our shores. Amen

Day 13

If any of you is without sin, let him be the first to throw a stone. John 8:7

Dear Lord,

Forgive us our insensitivity, our quick pointing finger and haughty criticisms. Hold us fast to genuine love, help us to look inward and recognize our own sinfulness. Teach us, that we might attend to our own inadequacies in lieu of condemning others. Amen

Day 14

Enter his gates with thanksgiving and his courts with praise.

Psalms 100:4

Dear Lord,

Please forgive us our ungratefulness. Continually remind us of how blessed we are with the gifts You have given. We live in an amazing country, full of beauty and full of freedom, yet so often we look only at what we do not have. Help us to look to You with thankful hearts, expressing gratitude for the provision You have so generously bestowed. Amen

Day 15

That you may be perfectly united in mind and thought.

1 Corinthians 1:10

Dear Lord,

Forgive us our faithlessness, our inability to turn to You as one. We vie for Your favor like small children, and we ask Your forgiveness for our inability to see the big picture. Please pull together the fragments of our country, that we might live, love and serve You as a community, as a nation. Amen

Day 16

Do not be overcome by evil, but overcome evil with good.

Romans 12:21

Dear Lord,

We thank You for our freedom to vote, to express our opinion in the government. Forgive us for not valuing this gift. Remind us of the blessing and help us, through this common voice, to bring Your will to pass. Amen

Day 17

Turn from evil and do good, seek peace and pursue it.

Psalms 34:14

Dear Lord,

We humbly ask for Your guidance in government. As the lawmakers join together to form the values we will stand for, let them do so with you as their guide. Amen

Day 18

All scripture is God-breathed.

2 Timothy 3:16

Dear Lord,

We thank You for the Bible, for the wisdom and teaching it imparts. Our forefathers based their lives on practicing these truths. Help us today to do the same, that we may take this living and breathing document and weave it into our lifestyles, corporately, as one.

Day 19

And whoever welcomes a little child like this in my name, welcomes me. Mathew 18:5

Dear Father,

We thank you for parents, for Mothers and Fathers. Help us to realize the weight of responsibility we carry in rearing our children. We humbly request Your encouragement, sustenance and vision for teaching what You wish us to convey to the tender hearts in our care. Amen

Day 20

Ensure your servants well being. Psalms 119:122

Dear Father,

We thank You for the police, for the men and women that daily lay their lives on the line so that we may know peace. Protect them with Your mighty hand, keep them from danger, and bless their commitment to serve. Amen

Day 21

So that all men may know of your mighty acts and the glorious splendor of your kingdom. Psalms 145:12

Dear Lord,

We thank You for firefighters, for those that enter the real heat of the flame to protect life and home. Father, may their spirit of volunteerism be a witness to all, that we might glorify You as we witness their commitment. Bless these heroes, Father. Please keep them safe. Amen

Day 22

If my people who are called by my name, will humble themselves and pray and seek my face... then will I hear from heaven and will forgive their sin and heal their land.

2 Chronicles 7:14

Dear Father,

We thank You for prayer, for the unique and wonderful opportunity we have to enter into Your presence daily. Forgive us for not humbling ourselves before You consistently. Help us to be diligent in prayer, that we would use such moments to seek Your face, ask Your forgiveness and respond to Your vision for this country. Amen

Day 23

She opens her arms to the poor and extends her hands to the needy. Proverbs 31:20

Dear Father,

Please bless the poor among us, help us to see them as You do, that we might give of ourselves and our resources willingly. Help us also to share our abundance with the poor all over the world. Let us serve in order that You might be glorified through our acts of kindness. Amen

Day 24

What God has joined together, let man not separate.

Mathew 19:6

Dear Father,

We are blessed by commitment. We bring You thanksgiving for marriages that are strong and true. The example they live out for us is priceless in value. Bless these unions Father, that they might continue to bring hope to others. Amen

Day 25

They will soar on wings like eagles.　　　Isaiah 40:31

Dear Lord,

We pray for those who have committed their service to the Air Force. The proud men and women who scan the darkened skies for any threat to our nation. Give them wings of eagles and safety in combat. We are grateful for their dedication. Amen

Day 26

For when I am weak, then I am strong.　　2 Corinthians 12:12

Dear Father,

So many of us are weak… physically, emotionally, spiritually. Strengthen us Father, transform our inadequacies with Your power and eternal perspective. Help us to lift one another up to the heights You have dreamed for us. Let us not look down on each other's differences, or condemn each other's weaknesses. Let us instead fully celebrate that Your plan for each life is perfect. Amen

Day 27

This will bring health to your body.　　　Proverbs 3:8

Dear Lord,

We thank You for this Nations hospitals, for the safe haven they provide to those that are sick and in need of help. Please bless these institutions, the staff that labor within them, and the healing their existence contributes to. Amen

Day 28

It was He who gave some to be apostles, some to be prophets, some to be evangelists and some to be pastors and teachers.

Ephesians 4:11

Dear Lord,

We thank You for our teachers, for those that place themselves in our schools with little financial reward. Grant them wisdom as they impart knowledge to the children in their care. Forgive us, as a country, for not valuing their contribution more and help us to understand the importance of their role in the lives of our children. Amen

Day 29

Is not wisdom found among the aged?   Job 12:12

Dear Father,

We thank You for the elderly, for their wisdom and insight into life's intricacies. Forgive us our callous indifference to their place in life, and help us to take the time to learn from their experiences. Ease them gently into their age Father, and let them know the joy that comes from relationship with You. Amen

Day 30

As Gods fellow workers, we urge you not to receive God's grace in vain.   2 Corinthians 6:1

Dear Lord,

We ask your forgiveness for our disobedience, for our willingness to bend your precepts to fit our own desires. Teach us and mold us Father, into a country that honors you first and foremost. Amen

Day 31

Will you not revive us again, that your people may rejoice in you?   Psalms 85:6

Dear Lord,

We get down on our knees and beg for revival. We ask You to sweep Your presence throughout this country. That every man, woman and child may know completeness in You. Help us to be ready for whatever call You may place on our lives. Whatever part we must play, let us do so willingly to bring all Nations to You. Amen

Deuteronomy 28:1-14 NCV

You must completely obey the LORD your God, and you must carefully follow all his commands I am giving you today. Then the LORD your God will make you greater than any other nation on earth. Obey the LORD your God so that all these blessings will come and stay with you:

You will be blessed in the city and blessed in the country.

Your children will be blessed, as well as your crops; your herds will be blessed with calves and your flocks with lambs.

Your basket and your kitchen will be blessed.

You will be blessed when you come in and when you go out.

The LORD will help you defeat the enemies that come to fight you. They will attack you from one direction, but they will run from you in seven directions.

The LORD your God will bless you with full barns, and he will bless everything you do. He will bless the land he is giving you.

The LORD will make you his holy people, as he promised. But you must obey his commands and do what he wants you to do. Then everyone on earth will see that you are the LORD's people, and they will be afraid of you. The LORD will make you rich: You will have many children, your animals will have many young, and your land will give good crops. It is the land that the LORD promised your ancestors he would give to you.

The LORD will open up his heavenly storehouse so that the skies send rain on your land at the right time, and he will bless everything you do. You will lend to other nations, but you will not need to borrow from them. The LORD will make you like the head and not like the tail; you will be on top and not on bottom. But you must obey the commands of the LORD your God that I am giving you today, being careful to keep them. Do not disobey anything I command you today. Do exactly as I command, and do not follow other gods or serve them.

God Bless America

By Irving Berlin

God Bless America,
Land that I love.
Stand beside her, and guide her
Through the night with a light from above.
From the mountains, to the prairies,
To the oceans, white with foam,
God bless America,
My home sweet home.

God bless America,
Land that I love.
Stand beside her,
And guide her,
Through the night
With the light from above.
From the mountains,
To the prairies,
To the ocean,
White with foam,
God bless America,
My home sweet home.
God bless America,
My home sweet home.

What Can You Do?

Write a Note

As we continue to pray for our nation and for those whose lives have been dramatically altered we ask you to take one more step. Enclosed is a postcard for you to write a personal note of encouragement or a prayer and send it to one of the following addresses:

The White House
1600 Pennsylvania Avenue NW
Washington, DC 20500

Governor George E. Pataki
State Capitol
Albany, NY 12224

Mayor Rudolph W. Giuliani
City Hall
New York, NY 10007

New York Fire Department
1 Chase Manhattan Plaza
New York, NY 10005

New York Police Department
16 Ericsson Place
New York, NY 10013

An individual you know serving in the armed forces or the newspaper they frequently read, Stars and Stripes.

Stars and Stripes
529 14th Street
NW Suite 350
Washington, DC 20045-1301

The victim's families in care of the following addresses:

Federal Emergency Management Association
500 C. Street SW, Rm 824
Washington, DC 20472-0001

American Red Cross
P.O. Box 37243
Washington, DC 20013

What Can You Do?

Donate Funds

Make a donation to a relief fund or charity of your choice. Contact your local Better Business Bureau for names and addresses of organizations.

On behalf of President Bush's request please help your children or children you know send a dollar to:

The Afghan Childrens Relief Fund
The White House
1600 Pennsylvania Avenue NW
Washington, DC 20500

Give Blood

Contact your local Red Cross for an appointment to give blood. And continue to give blood on a regular basis.

Pray

Take time to pray each day. Create a prayer group at your church to pray for our country's leaders and military forces. (See II Timothy 2:1,2) If you would like to join the presidential prayer team go to: www.PresidentialPrayerTeam.org

Send Us Your Story

Send us your inspirational story or prayer to our website: www.americaoutoftheashes.com

Met in the Stairwell

You say you will never forget where you were when you heard the news, September 11, 2001. Neither will I.

I was on the 110th floor in a smoke filled room with a man who called his wife to say "Good-bye." I held his fingers steady as he dialed. I gave him the peace to say, "Honey, I am not going to make it, but it is OK . . . I am ready to go." I was with his wife when he called as she fed breakfast to their children. I held her up as she tried to understand his words and as she realized he wasn't coming home that night.

I was in the stairwell of the 23rd floor when a woman cried out to Me for help. "I have been knocking on the door of your heart for 50 years!", I said. "Of course I will show you the way home—only believe on Me now."

I was at the base of the building with the Priest ministering to the injured and devastated souls. I took him home to tend to his flock in Heaven. He heard My voice and answered.

I was on all four of those planes, in every seat, with every prayer. I was with the crew as they were overtaken.

I was in the very hearts of the believers there. Comforting and assuring them that their faith has saved them.

I was in Texas, Kansas, London. I was standing next to you when you heard the terrible news. Did you sense Me?

I want you to know that I saw every face. I knew every name-though they did NOT all know Me. Some met Me for the first time on the 100th floor. Some sought Me out in their last breath. Some couldn't hear Me calling to them throughout the smoke and flames, "Come to Me . . . this way . . . take my hand." Some chose, for the final time, to ignore Me. But, I was there.

I did not place you in the Tower that day—you may not know why, But I DO. However, if you were there in that explosive moment in time, would you have reached for Me? September 11, 2001, was not the end of the journey for you. But someday your journey will end. And I will be there for you as well. Seek Me now while I may be found. Then, at any moment, you know you are "ready to go." I will be in the stairwell of your final moments.

GOD
(Author Unknown)

Behold, I stand at the door, and knock:
if any man hear my voice, and open
the door, I will come in to him, and
will sup with him, and he with me.

Revelation 3:20

Additional copies of this book
and other titles from Honor Books
are available at your local bookstore.

If this book has impacted your life,
we would like to hear from you.

Please contact us at:

Honor Books
Department E
P.O. Box 55388
Tulsa, Oklahoma 74155
Or by e-mail at info@honorbooks.com

www.americaoutoftheashes.com